Vorwort

Mit dem neuen, spannenden Compact Lernkrimi können Sie Ihre Englischkenntnisse auf schnelle und einfache Weise vertiefen, auffrischen und überprüfen.
Inspector Hudson erleichtert das Sprachtraining mit Action und Humor. Er und seine mysteriösen Kriminalfälle stehen im Mittelpunkt einer zusammenhängenden Story.
Der Krimi wird auf jeder Seite durch abwechslungsreiche und kurzweilige Übungen ergänzt, die das Lernen unterhaltsam und spannend machen.
Prüfen Sie Ihr Englisch in Lückentexten, Zuordnungs- und Übersetzungsaufgaben, in Buchstabenspielen und Kreuzworträtseln!
Ob im Bus oder in der Bahn, im Wartezimmer, zu Hause oder in der Mittagspause – das Sprachtraining im handlichen Format bietet die ideale Trainingsmöglichkeit für zwischendurch.
Schreiben Sie die Lösungen einfach ins Buch!
Die richtigen Antworten sind in einem eigenen Lösungsteil zusammengefasst.

Und nun kann die Spannung beginnen …

Viel Spaß und Erfolg!

Inhalt

Story

James Hudson arbeitet als Inspector bei der legendären Polizeibehörde Scotland Yard. Er ist einer der fähigsten Männer und wird immer dann zu Rate gezogen, wenn seine Kollegen mal wieder vor einem Rätsel stehen. Seine resolute und krimibegeisterte Haushälterin Miss Paddington unterstützt ihn stets mit liebevoller Fürsorge. Und insgeheim verfolgt sie noch ein weiteres Ziel: ihn endlich mit der jungen, attraktiven Versicherungsagentin Elvira Elliot zu verkuppeln.

In einer Londoner Nobelgalerie werden auf unerklärliche Weise drei Gemälde gestohlen: Ein Monet, ein Picasso sowie ein unbedeutendes Portrait des längst verstorbenen Lord Ploughbuttom.
Hudson kann sich zunächst keinen Reim darauf machen.
Was verbirgt sich hinter dem Bildnis des Lords?
Welche Rolle spielt das international gesuchte Phantom in dem mysteriösen Fall? Wird es gelingen, den Unbekannten zu fassen?
Nach und nach gelingt es Inspector Hudson, Licht in das Dunkel des Unerklärlichen zu bringen …

The Mysterious Painting

Inspector James Hudson stared at the pile of files in front of him and sighed.

Scotland Yard was a world famous institution – and an immense bureaucracy.

During the past few weeks, James Hudson had solved dozens of cases. He had cleared up the mystery of a disappeared mummy, exposed a supposed 'hell-hound' as a fraud and brought over half-a-dozen criminals behind bars.

However, the paperwork for the cases were a long way from being closed. In front of him were piles of reports, petitions, protocols to be signed and evaluations. The forms in which the officers were supposed to write a short press release about the cases solved were particularly annoying.

Übung 1: Welche Zeit- und Mengeneinheit wird beschrieben?

ÜBUNG 1 !

1. 24 hours ____________________
2. seven days ____________________
3. thirty minutes ____________________
4. about thirty days ____________________
5. twelve of the same objects ____________________
6. sixty minutes ____________________
7. 365 days ____________________

Sir Reginald, Hudson's boss, had initiated these forms, in order to improve relations between the Yard and the press.

Inspector Hudson did not think much of this sort of public relations. In addition, these press releases meant more work, which kept him from his real job – solving crimes.

To avoid the paperwork a little longer, Hudson stood up and watered the sick plant standing on the windowsill of the small, undecorated office.

Then he sat down on his creaky chair and took the first file from the pile.

The telephone rang.

Hudson glanced at the number on the display. A few weeks ago, he finally received a digital telephone connection. Modern technology actually had its advantages.

Hudson picked up the receiver.

ÜBUNG 2 !

Übung 2: Wie heißt das Wort auf Englisch?

1. Haufen/Menge __________
2. seufzen __________
3. Betrug __________
4. Rätsel __________
5. Gutachten __________
6. nervig/unangenehm __________
7. Fall __________
8. vermeiden __________
9. Akte __________

"Good morning, Sir Reginald," he said. "What can I do for you?"

"Morning, Hudson," barked Sir Reginald into the receiver. Hudson's boss reminded him of a bulldog, not only because of his looks – but also because of the way he spoke. "Are you in the middle of something important?"

Inspector Hudson glanced at the pile on his desk.

"No, sir. I have plenty of time."

"Good – then come to my office."

"With pleasure," answered Hudson. "May I ask what it is …?"

But Sir Reginald had already slammed down the receiver.

Hudson smiled and put the file back on the pile.

One minute later, James Hudson was knocking on his boss' door.

A voice barked, "Come in!"

Hudson straightened his tie one more time and opened the door. Sir Reginald was standing behind his desk and holding telephone receivers to both ears.

Somehow he was able to conduct two conversations at the same time, and he didn't seem to be in a very good mood. He motioned Hudson to take a seat in the visitor's chair in front of his desk.

Hudson sat down and observed with amusement that his boss, Sir Reginald, was able to end both telephone conversations simultaneously.

Übung 3: Welches Wort ist das „schwarze Schaf"?

ÜBUNG 3 !

1. boss, supervisor, worker, head ____________

2. plenty, few, many, a lot ____________

3. smile, grin, smirk, frown ____________

4. one after the other, both, at once, together ____________

5. mood, feeling, knowledge, emotion ____________

6. cold, flu, healthy, infection ____________

7. lacking, enough, adequate, sufficient ____________

"This cursed flu!" growled Sir Reginald.
"Excuse me, sir, are you not well?"
Sir Reginald shook his head. "Oh no. I'm fine. Great! But half of my department is flat on its back. We don't have enough personnel."

ÜBUNG 4 !

Übung 4: Unterstreichen Sie das Substantiv im Text!
(1. Epidemie 2. Immunsystem 3. Routinefall 4. Weisheit 5. Tatort)

Hudson nodded. A serious flu epidemic was sweeping through London. Miss Paddington, Hudson's housekeeper, had been bothering him for days with hot lemon and chicken soup, to strengthen his immune system, as she said. Till now, she had been very successful.
"That's why I called you here, Hudson," continued Sir Reginald. "Are you working on any important cases right now?"
The inspector thought about the pile of files on his desk and shook his head.
"Nothing that can't wait, sir."
"Very good. Very good. Then I would like to give you a new case. A routine case – no mummies and hell-hounds this time."
Inspector James Hudson nodded. Without wanting to, he had become an expert for unsolved cases within the Yard. Whenever

his colleagues were at their wit's end, he would be summoned to the scene of the crime.

"Of course, sir. May I ask what it is about?"
"Last night there was a burglary at the Blighton-Gallery, do you know what that is?"
"Well sir, as far as I know, a burglary refers to the forced opening of a lock that is not supposed to be opened, with the intention of taking another's property."
"Very funny," growled Sir Reginald. "You are developing a sense of humour on the job, Hudson. That is suspicious. Very suspicious."
Sir Reginald forced a smile and poured the inspector a cup of tea.

Übung 5: Welches englische Wort wird beschrieben?

ÜBUNG 5 !

1. Das Möbelstück, auf dem man mit dem PC arbeitet.

   computer table

2. Jemand, der sehr viel über etwas weiß.

   ____

3. Menschen, mit denen man zusammenarbeitet.

   ____

4. Eine Tat, die gegen die Gesetze verstößt.

   ____

5. Ein Beruf, bei dem man Haus und Hof versorgt.

   ____

6. Der Teil des Telefons, den man abhebt, um zu sprechen.

____

"But seriously, Hudson. Do you know the Blighton-Gallery?"
"Isn't it the small art gallery in the centre, sir?" asked the inspector. Sir Reginald nodded.
"Exactly. Small, but very exclusive. And expensive. Doctors and lawyers buy paintings there for decorating their offices. Very rich doctors and lawyers."

ÜBUNG 6 !

Übung 6: Wie heißt der Beruf auf Englisch?

1. Privatdetektiv ______________________________
2. Polizist ______________________________
3. Anwalt ______________________________
4. Buchhalter ______________________________
5. Schriftsteller ______________________________
6. Kunsthändler ______________________________
7. Richter ______________________________
8. Versicherungsvertreter ______________________________
9. Auktionator ______________________________

Hudson glanced behind Sir Reginald. On the wall hung a scrawled portrait of Sir Reginald that his granddaughter had made for him a few months ago. Sir Reginald had proudly showed it around the entire department.

Sir Reginald observed the inspector's gaze.
"Well. I like it better than a Picasso. But, while we're on the subject – the thieves stole a Picasso and a painting by Monet, and some old thing. I forgot by whom."
Sir Reginald shuffled around in his papers – with no success.
"It doesn't matter. The paintings were worth millions. I want you to take care of this, Hudson."
The inspector frowned.
"Stolen art is not exactly my cup of tea, sir. I have to admit, if you had told me, that the portrait behind you was by Picasso and not by your granddaughter, I would have believed you."

Übung 7: Ordnen Sie die Verben richtig zu!
Welche Wörter gehören wohin?

ÜBUNG 7 !

a) to protect nature b) to cross oneself c) to go sightseeing d) to book e) to delete a file f) to conceive a child g) to be baptised h) to go on strike

1. Biologie ____________________

2. Religion ____________________

3. Tourismus ____________________

4. Arbeitswelt ____________________

Sir Reginald rolled his eyes.
"Don't try to be funny again, Hudson. Normally I would have given the case to Inspector Wilson, but he's in bed with a fever. You will have to take over, for better or for worse."

Hudson stood up.
"Of course, sir. I'm afraid that I don't know much about art."
"Don't worry, Hudson. As far as I know, a civilian expert is already investigating at the scene. You can work together and exchange information."
Hudson was just about to say something more when one of the telephones rang, and then the other one.

ÜBUNG 8

Übung 8: Setzen Sie die richtige Präposition ein!

While Sir Reginald held both receivers 1. ________ his ears and barked into the mouthpieces, Inspector Hudson left the office quietly and thoughtfully. A 'civilian expert'? Who could that possibly be?

"You?!" cried Inspector Hudson.
He stood 2. __________ the exhibit room of the Blighton-Gallery and stared with astonishment 3. ________ Elvira Elliot, the young insurance agent.
Elvira brushed a strand of blazing red hair out of her face and smiled at the inspector.
"James, I'm happy to see you, too. Who would have thought that we would work together again? I was afraid that Sir Reginald would have put that bore Wilson 4. ________ the case."
"Wilson is sick," replied the inspector, "I am handling the case."

"Well thank God," said Elvira.

Hudson gulped. It was true that he liked Elvira Elliot and had often worked 5. __________ her. However, when the young insurance agent showed up at the scene of the crime, it meant one thing: trouble …

Elvira yanked the inspector out of his thoughts.

"Come on, James, let's look 6. ________ before your colleagues 7. ________ the forensics department destroy all the evidence."

Hudson looked around. At least half-a-dozen men and women hurried through the roomy gallery. They took finger prints, examined doors and windows for traces and questioned a man, who was sitting stunned on a chair.
This had to be Mr Blighton, the gallery's owner.
Blighton answered a young policeman's questions and repeatedly glanced at the opposite wall. Two light squares indicated that the stolen paintings had recently hung here.
The inspector glanced around. On the other walls of the modern gallery, were dozens of paintings. Even the inspector, who was no expert on art, recognised some of them.
Mr Blighton had been kind enough not to put price tags on his pictures. The inspector was sure, that his year's salary would not be enough to buy even one of the frames.
Elvira seemed to read his mind.
"The paintings you are looking at, James, are easily worth a few million pounds. Both stolen paintings, the Monet and the Picasso, alone are estimated between two and three million pounds."

The inspector was startled. Hadn't Sir Reginald mentioned three paintings?

"Why *two* paintings, Elvira?" he asked.

The insurance agent smirked.

"These stupid thieves took a portrait of an old English aristocrat along with the Picasso and the Monet. At best, the portrait has a certain sentimental value, but it is not worth nearly as much as the other paintings."

Elvira took a glossy brochure from a small table and opened it. Then she showed the inspector the pages with the stolen paintings. Hudson nodded. Both pictures – a crazy Picasso and a colourful Monet – were exquisite – as were their prices.

Inspector Hudson felt dizzy as he looked at the prices. He had not been mistaken in his estimate of the paintings' value.

"Not bad," said the inspector, without specifying if he meant the paintings or their prices.

ÜBUNG 9 !

Übung 9: Spiegelt der Satz den richtigen Sachverhalt wider? Markieren Sie: richtig ✓ falsch –

1. The light, square spots on the gallery walls showed where new paintings were going to be hung.
2. Some of the paintings in the gallery were familiar to Hudson.
3. Hudson thought he could afford many of the paintings.
4. The stolen paintings were worth a lot of money.
5. Only two paintings were stolen.
6. The third painting was worth as much as the Picasso and the Monet.
7. At least one of the paintings was of a person.

"That's right," replied Elvira as she flipped through the catalogue. The third painting was on one of the last pages, much smaller than the famous paintings at the beginning. The price was also pretty affordable.

I would have to sell my old Bentley to have this hanging in my living room, thought the inspector. But he didn't see any reason to.

Übung 10: Unterstreichen Sie die Verben und bilden Sie die Grundform!

ÜBUNG 10 !

The painting was of a man in his thirties dressed in old-fashioned clothes. The young man, obviously a lord, stared at the observer with a mysterious smile. A stray dark curl fell on the aristocratic forehead.

The portrait was solidly executed but, as far as the inspector could tell, just a standard portrait of an aristocrat – one of many thousands in England. The only thing remarkable were the two dices the young lord held in his left hand. Both showed a six.

"*Portrait of Lord Ploughbottom*" was the title given in the catalogue, "*late 17th century, anonymous.*"

Elvira shut the catalogue.

"There is a reason the artist is anonymous," she said with a wrinkle of her nose.

As an insurance agent, it was obvious that Elvira knew more about art than Hudson. She was probably constantly involved in cases of disappearing artworks.

Inspector Hudson stroked his chin thoughtfully. Either the mysterious thieves were badly informed or they had taken the wrong painting in their hurry.

ÜBUNG 11 !

Übung 11: Wie heißt das Verb im Simple Past?

1. suspect — suspected
2. mug ____________________
3. strike ____________________
4. rape ____________________
5. smuggle ____________________
6. seek out ____________________
7. take revenge ____________________
8. kidnap ____________________
9. rob ____________________
10. hijack ____________________
11. swear ____________________
12. find a clue ____________________
13. dig ____________________
14. cling ____________________

"Do we know how the thieves entered the building?" asked Hudson. He was embarrassed to ask Elvira, but the insurance agent had arrived before him at the scene of the crime. And Hudson was sure that Elvira had already pumped the forensics team for information. Elvira Elliot shrugged her shoulders.

Übung 12: Finden Sie das Synonym für die Wörter im Text!
(1. modern 2. trace 3. examine 4. broken 5. unhurt 6. unusual)

"Your colleagues have absolutely no idea, James. The Blighton-Gallery has the most up-to-date security system possible. But the thieves seemed to have just waltzed in and out without leaving any trace."
"Impossible." The inspector shook his head. "There is always a clue … there must be a clue. One just has to know where to look for it."
Hudson began to inspect the gallery's windows. The exhibit rooms were on the ground floor; therefore, it was possible that the robbers came through one of the windows.
But Elvira was right: The window panes had not been damaged and no-one had tampered with the alarm wiring.
A quick inspection showed that the entrance door was also unharmed.
"This is very strange," murmured the inspector. The thieves must have gained access to the building somehow.

Elvira Elliot glanced suspiciously at Mr Blighton, the gallery owner, who was still cowered in a corner.
"Maybe it's an insurance fraud," she muttered.
Inspector Hudson shook his head.
"I don't think so, Elvira. If Mr Blighton or someone else had only faked the theft, they would have left some clues, in order to divert suspicion from themselves."
"That is a good point," nodded Elvira Elliot, almost a little disappointed.
Hudson looked around.
"Are there any back rooms?" he asked.

Übung 13: Finden Sie die Wortverbindungen!

1.	police	☐	colour
2.	keep under	☐	paint
3.	bank	☐	brigade
4.	genetic	☐	clothes
5.	protection	☐	robber
6.	diplomatic	☐	force
7.	secret	☐	relation
8.	in civilian	☐	shot
9.	pistol	☐	observation
10.	code	☐	treaty
11.	sign a	☐	name
12.	fire	☐	fingerprint
13.	picture	☐	agent
14.	oil	☐	mony
15.	water	☐	frame
16.	pastel	☐	crayon

The insurance agent pointed to a hall at the other end of the exhibition room.
"Yes, a salon, Mr Blighton's office and the bathroom. But none of these rooms have windows or doors."
"Mmm. Nevertheless, I would like to see them," answered Hudson and crossed the exhibition hall.
Elvira followed him.
Hudson was deep in thought.
As a young and unexperienced police officer, he was forced to learn that crimes and crime scenes were never one-dimensional – in every sense of the word.

Übung 14: Beantworten Sie die Fragen zum Text!

ÜBUNG 14 !

1. Why was Elvira Elliot also involved in the case?

2. What is Lord Ploughbottom holding in his hand?

3. Which famous artists painted two of the stolen pictures?

4. Why was it strange that the portrait of Lord Ploughbottom was taken as well?

5. Who painted the portrait of Lord Ploughbottom?

6. What part of the crime was confusing Elvira and Hudson ?

With a shudder, the inspector remembered one of his first cases: the hunt for a spiderwoman. Ever since then, he had accustomed himself to look at all three dimensions of a crime scene: not only the floor, but also the ceiling, and also what was under the floor. In order to keep any fingerprints intact, the inspector pulled a handkerchief out of his jacket pocket and opened the door to the salon carefully. He took a look inside. Elvira Elliot peeped over his shoulder.

Nothing. The elegantly decorated room was untouched – and had neither windows nor doors leading to the outside.

Hudson repeated the same procedure with Mr Blighton's office. Apart from the fact that Inspector Hudson had never seen such an elegantly furnished and neat office, there was nothing out of the ordinary.

Only the bathroom remained.

Without much hope, the inspector turned the doorknob and looked inside. His eyes widened.

"Oh my goodness!" cried Elvira Elliot.

Übung 15: Wie heißt der Satz auf Deutsch? Kreuzen Sie die richtige Übersetzung an!

1. Elvira followed him.
   - a) ☐ Elvira folgt ihm.
   - b) ☐ Elvira wäre ihm gefolgt.
   - c) ☐ Elvira folgte ihm.

2. He had accustomed himself of considering every aspect.
   - a) ☐ Er wird sich daran gewöhnen, jeden Aspekt zu berücksichtigen.
   - b) ☐ Er hatte sich daran gewöhnt, jeden Aspekt zu berücksichtigen.
   - c) ☐ Er konnte sich daran gewöhnen, jeden Aspekt zu berücksichtigen.

3. The inspector pulls a handkerchief out of his pocket.
   - a) ☐ Der Inspektor zog ein Taschentuch aus seiner Tasche.
   - b) ☐ Der Inspektor zieht ein Taschentuch aus seiner Tasche.
   - c) ☐ Der Inspektor hat ein Taschentuch aus seiner Tasche gezogen.

4. There will be nothing out of the ordinary.
   a) ☐ Es gäbe nichts Außerordentliches.
   b) ☐ Es gab nichts Außerordentliches.
   c) ☐ Es wird nichts Außerordentliches geben.

5. Only the bathroom remained.
   a) ☐ Nur das Bad wurde frei.
   b) ☐ Nur die Badewanne blieb übrig.
   c) ☐ Nur das Badezimmer blieb noch übrig.

The bathroom looked like a construction site following a bomb explosion. The sinks were torn from the walls and lay shattered on the floor. A large part of the tiles were destroyed. The most astonishing thing was the huge hole that gaped in the middle of the floor. It was at least two metres wide. A few broken pipes stuck out at the rim like bent branches.

"What happened here?" Elvira gasped.

Inspector Hudson took a few steps forward. Broken ceramic pieces crunched under his feet.

He peered into the hole in the floor. It was so deep that one couldn't see the bottom.

"Here we are, Elvira, my dear," the inspector said and let loose a long breath. "We are looking at the way that the thieves used to get into the gallery after visiting hours."

"You can say that again," replied Elvira. She also took a look at the hole in the floor.

"My goodness. They were diligent. It must take days to dig a tunnel like this."

Hudson nodded thoughtfully. Something was really bothering him.

"That also means," continued Elvira, "that the thieves must have begun digging the tunnel nearby. If we are lucky, somewhere close."

ÜBUNG 16 !

Übung 16: Setzen Sie die Sätze ins Passiv!

1. He destroyed the painting.

   The painting was destroyed by him.

2. The thieves tore the sinks from the walls.

   ___

3. Hudson inspected the hole.

   ___

4. Elvira moved the tiles.

   ___

5. Mr Blighton sees the damage.

   ___

6. The inspector takes notes.

   ___

The inspector shook his head. “Hmmm,” was all he said.
Elvira put her hands on her hips.
“James, don’t start with that ‘hmm’. You have some suspicion or other. Am I right?”
The inspector glanced at Elvira and nodded.
“This reminds me of a case that I had many years ago. I was wondering if … ”
Without finishing his sentence, the inspector began to climb into the hole. Elvira stared at him with wide eyes.
“James! What are you doing? It’s too dangerous.”

Übung 17: Wie heißt das Wort auf Deutsch?

1.	climb	☐	feucht
2.	hole	☐	Taschenlampe
3.	dangerous	☐	klebrig
4.	chute	☐	Loch
5.	flashlight	☐	folgen
6.	follow	☐	gefährlich
7.	damp	☐	vertraut
8.	sticky	☐	Schacht
9.	familiar	☐	klettern

Inspector Hudson descended a bit lower. His searching feet found a stable hold on the chute's wall.

Then he slowly shook his head.

"I don't think so. The thieves were kind enough to carve little notches in the chute's wall. Do you see?"

Hudson climbed a bit lower to demonstrate.

Übung 18: Setzen Sie das richtige Wort ein!

"I want to take a look at this little construction before the (1. Gerichtsmedizin) __________ people take notice and trample all of the (2. Anhaltspunkte) __________ with their flat feet."

Elvira did not hesitate for a moment.

"You're right," she whispered (3. verschwörerisch) __________ and quietly shut the door to the bathroom.

(4. dann) ______________ she pulled a small flashlight out of her purse and followed the inspector into the hole.

Climbing down was easy.

They only needed a minute to reach the end of the horizontal chute. The (5. Lichtstrahl) _________ of Elvira's flashlight showed another chute. It was so narrow that they had no (6. Wahl) _____ _____ but to crawl.

"Can I use your flashlight?" the inspector asked and crept (7. nach vorne) ___________ after Elvira gave it to him.

The cramped chute was damp and sticky. The air smelled like mould – and something else that the inspector was familiar with.
"Do you smell that?" he asked while moving forward.
"Smells like mould," she said with disgust. "I hate to think about how my designer dress will look when we come out again. But you're right. I smell something else too, but I can't tell what."
"If my hunch is correct," answered Hudson, "then we should find out immediately."
Hudson noticed that the chute didn't run horizontally anymore, but slightly curved. It couldn't be far off now.
All of a sudden, the flashlight's beam was swallowed up in a huge opening. Elvira froze.
"What's that?" she asked with amazement.
The inspector stood up without difficulty. The small passage had merged into a tunnel, about ten metres high, which seemed to go on forever. Small calcium stalactites shone from the ceiling.

Übung 19: Setzen Sie das richtige Verb ein! ***(zögern, krabbeln, zertrampeln, um Hilfe bitten, scheinen, riechen)***

1. Hudson ______________ Elvira ______________.
2. The thieves ______________ on the paintings and ruined them.
3. Hudson could ______________ the fresh coffee.
4. The sun did not ______________ into the dark tunnel.
5. Elvira ______________ because she did not want to go in.
6. The tunnel was so low that he had to ____________ through it.

A dark shadow – probably a huge rat – slithered over a rusty piece of metal on the ground.

The inspector showed the flashlight around.

"This, my dear, is one of the many underground lines in London no longer in use. The entire city is connected by a network of these lines, like Swiss cheese, so to say. That's why the smell was familiar – it reminds me of the scent of a normal underground tunnel – only here it is much stronger."

Elvira made a face.

"You can say that again," she nodded.

"These tunnels were dug at the beginning of the last century," Hudson explained. "Several of them became part of the modern underground network that we know. Many others – like this one – were simply forgotten."

"Obviously not by everybody," remarked Elvira. "I bet the thieves knew that this tunnel runs by the Blighton-Gallery – and took advantage of their knowledge."

Hudson nodded.

Übung 20: Finden Sie die englische Entsprechung der folgenden Adverbien und Adjektive im Text!
(direkt, genau, endlich, alt, dunkel, schmal, enorm, verwüstet, sprachlos)

"It looks that way. Unfortunately. The criminals could have entered the old tunnel from anywhere …"

"… and strolled through the chambers …"

"… and dug their way up directly under the gallery."

Elvira looked at the inspector with frustration.

"That means, we are back to square one." Elvira's sighs echoed through the dark tunnel.

"Not exactly," replied Hudson and pointed to the narrow chute through which they had come.

"Let's go back to the surface. I may have an idea how we can proceed."

The police inspector and the insurance agent crawled back through the narrow chute and re-entered the huge crater in the gallery. The other police officers had in the meantime noticed the inspector's disappearance and finally had discovered the hole in the wash room.

They gaped at Hudson and Elliot's clay smeared clothes as the two emerged from the hole.

The inspector dusted the worst of the dirt from his jacket and slapped one of the officers on the back.

"We just looked around a little bit, old boy."

Then he and Elliot left the wasted bathroom.

The forensics team remained speechless as they watched them go.

Übung 21: Bringen Sie die Wörter in die richtige Reihenfolge!

ÜBUNG 21 !

1. hunch correct Hudson's was

____

2. floor the rat is A crawling across

____

3. a does flashlight He have not

____

4. is dangerous tunnel The

____

5. destroyed Who the bathroom?

____

6. everyone Scotland Yard Almost flu the has at

____

Miss Paddington looked worriedly at the sofa, on which Hudson and Elliot had sat down, still in their dirty clothes. But her maternal instinct got the better of her.

"Would you like another cup of tea?" asked Miss Paddington and poured Elvira another cup before she could answer.

"That is very kind of you, Miss Paddington. Thank you very much."

After their little excursion underground, Hudson had insisted that Elvira accompanies him to his little house in Baker Street.

Although on the way there Elvira had often tried to get him to answer her many questions, Hudson had remained silent. Something was obviously bothering him.

ÜBUNG 22 !

Übung 22: Welches Wort ist das „schwarze Schaf"?

1. house, flat, garage, cottage ____________________

2. question, inquiry, query, reply ____________________

3. painting, sculpture, picture, portrait ____________________

4. safe, dangerous, risky, hazardous ____________________

5. peacefull, tranquill, calm, nervous ____________________

6. gallery, bar, museum, showroom ____________________

7. sip, gulp, swallow, spit ____________________

Elvira took a sip of the steaming Earl Grey tea – Hudson's favourite – and made another effort.

"OK, James. What is it that you absolutely wanted to show me? I don't want to rush, and I would be happy to accept an invitation from you to tea anytime – but there is a crime waiting to be solved," she said, slightly impatient.

ÜBUNG 23 !

Übung 23: Übersetzen Sie!

1. Darf ich Ihnen ein Kompliment machen?

____

2. Sie sehen heute bezaubernd aus.

____

3. Wie wär's mit etwas zu essen?

____

4. Auf dein Wohl!

____

The inspector tranquilly took a sip of tea.
"It's for exactly that reason that we're here. Be patient, Elvira."
Hudson glanced at his housekeeper.
"Miss Paddington. Do you remember Jimmy Coltrane? He had the pleasure of being our guest for a few days?"
Miss Paddington huffed.
"Do I remember Jimmy Coltrane? And how I remember that good-for-nothing! He ate half of the pantry and had terrible manners."
Hudson chuckled to himself. As far as he could remember, Miss Paddington and old Jimmy had got along very well – their constant sparring was just a joke.
"Who the hell is Jimmy Coltrane?" asked Elvira.
One didn't need to be a detective to figure out that her patience was wearing thin.

Übung 24: Bilden Sie das englische Wort aus dem Buchstabenchaos! !

ÜBUNG 24

1. CERUIXNOS (Ausflug) ______________
2. PACNOAYMC (begleiten) ______________
3. ANRMIE (verbleiben) ______________
4. EBHROT (stören) ______________
5. CFSRAUE (Oberfläche) ______________

6. COESINRSF (Spurensicherung) ____________________

7. RTAEMLAN (mütterlich) ____________________

8. TIITINOVNA (Einladung) ____________________

9. SNENRAM (Manieren) ____________________

10. TIPAMNTIE (ungeduldig) ____________________

Miss Paddington waved her hand dismissively.
"An insignificant thief." Obviously she didn't want to expand on the topic.
"A very talented thief," contradicted Hudson. Then he turned to Elvira.
"Jimmy was one of my first cases, many years ago. He was a small-time crook, who had got a hold of old underground maps. Not maps of the current network that you can get anywhere, but an entire directory of all the tunnels no longer in use."
Elvira ears perked up.
"Jimmy Coltrane got a gang of professionals together and used the old underground tunnels to dig into half a dozen banks."

ÜBUNG 25 !

Übung 25: Vervollständigen Sie die Wortverbindungen!
(gang, glass, sum, ray, pound, clump, gust, spot, sip, piece)

1. a ______________ of tea

2. a ______________ of thieves

3. a ______________ of money

4. a ______________ of advice

5. a ____________ of dirt

6. a ____________ of paint

7. a ____________ of wine

8. a ____________ of butter

9. a ____________ of wind

10. a ____________ of light

The inspector took another sip of tea and ignored Miss Paddington shaking her head.
"Jimmy did one robbery after another and we may have never caught him. Unfortunately, during one of his hunts, he ran into London's Mole-Men."
"Mole-Men?" asked Elvira uncomprehendingly.

Übung 26: Setzen Sie die Verben ein!
(looked, fastened, seemed, make out, stared, exist, fought)

Hudson, Elvira and Miss Paddington (1. blicken) ____________ up at the yellowed underground maps, that the inspector had (2. festmachen) ____________ on the living room wall. The large, musty smelling maps showed a complicated network of lines, that (3. scheinen) ____________ to go nowhere. Only after examining them more closely, could they (4. erkennen) __________ a system. Even Miss Paddington, who at first was only concerned for the wallpaper, (5. starren) ____________ at the maps with fascination. "Fascinating, isn't it?" asked the inspector. "Like a lost world. The underground has snaked through London since 1863, and many of the old lines don't run anymore. Back then, the underground was not the sole property of the City of London. A half-a-dozen private companies (6. kämpfen) ______________ for dominance – and many companies lost their routes.

All total, there are more than 40 so-called 'ghost stations' in London, abandoned stations, some that haven't been used in over 100 years."
Elvira took a step forward and examined the map.
"True," she murmured mesmerised and pointed to the map, "I don't know some of these routes at all."
Then her gaze darkened.
"But James, if there are 40 abandoned underground stations, then there are 40 places as well, in which the thieves could have entered the tunnel system. How can we find the right station?"
The inspector smiled at Elvira encouragingly.

ÜBUNG 27

Übung 27: Trifft die Aussage zu? Markieren Sie: richtig ✓ falsch –

1. If something is yellowed, it is usually old.
2. Miss Paddington was not interested in the maps.
3. All of the underground routes in Inspector Hudson's maps are still in use.
4. If something is abandoned, it is no longer being used.

5. Many of the 'ghost stations' are in the suburbs.
6. Jimmy Coltrane used the maps of the underground system to sell drugs.
7. Jimmy Coltrane never went to jail.
8. Jimmy Coltrane was very kind to Miss Paddington and Mr Hudson.
9. Some of the abandoned stations in London are over 100 years old.
10. Hudson thought it would be difficult to find the place where the thieves entered the tunnel system.

"It's not as hard as it seems, my dear Elvira. A large part of the 'ghost stations' are in the centre of the city, in the middle of business areas full of people. Of course these can be excluded. In addition, land is extremely scarce in London, which means that many of the old stations have been torn down and built over a long time ago." Elvira nodded.

Übung 28: Setzen Sie die Wörter ein!
(ghost, replaced, middle, perfect, network, entrance, building, snapped, notice, particular)

ÜBUNG 28 !

"Then only a few of the 1. '____________ stations' are outside of the centre."

The inspector shook his head. "Not necessarily. I have one 2. ____________ station in mind. This one here."

Hudson used a pencil to point to a spot on the map. It was at a point, where the 3. ____________ was most interconnected.

Miss Paddington, who had until now remained quiet, staring at the map, said, "are you sure, James? That is in the 4. ____________ of the city, next to the British Museum, if I am not mistaken. Wouldn't somebody 5. ____________ when a gang of thieves were running around with jack hammers and picks?"

Hudson nodded.

"You are absolutely right, Miss Paddington. Until 1933, there was a station at the British Museum. It was removed and 6. ____________ with the neighbouring station, Holborn. However, this old 7. ____________ would have been 8. ____________ for thieves with shovels and picks."

"And why is that?" asked Elvira, astonished.

"It's very simple, my dear. Because an office 9. ____________ is currently being constructed on this site. You have certainly seen the construction site."

Elvira 10. ____________ her fingers.

"You're right, James," she cried. "I remember now. The building is even for one of our subsidiaries. On such a large construction site, nobody would notice a few extra people with digging equipment!"

"Exactly," replied Hudson. "And tonight, I am going to take a look at this site."
"I'll go with you!" cried Elvira, without hesitation, but the inspector merely shook his head.
"Honestly, Elvira, I would prefer it, if you would ask around in the art scene. Maybe the theft of the two paintings …"
"Three," corrected Elvira.
"… *three* paintings, was a hired theft. Perhaps a fanatical art collector hired the thieves especially for this coup! You know much more about the scene than I do, Elvira."
Elvira was thoughtful for a moment, then nodded.
"You're right, James, that makes sense. I will get to work at once."

Übung 29: Wie heißt der Plural der folgenden Substantive?

1. thief ____________________
2. scene ____________________
3. half ____________________
4. mouse ____________________
5. wolf ____________________
6. light ____________________
7. tunnel ____________________
8. loaf ____________________

Elvira grabbed her handbag and gave the inspector a quick kiss on the cheek.
"Take care of yourself, James," she whispered.

The inspector blushed. Miss Paddington smiled to herself. For years, she had been trying to bring the confirmed bachelor and the attractive insurance agent together. One day she would be successful.

"Uhhm, right," stammered the inspector, after Elvira had gone. "I am going to make a few preparations for tonight."

While Miss Paddington grinned, the inspector fled up the narrow steps to the first floor and disappeared into his room.

A few hours later, the sun had already set, and Miss Paddington was at the stove, sizzling a hearty supper for the inspector.

If James was going to be hunting crooks in the middle of the night, then at least he can do it on a full stomach, she thought.

Suddenly, Miss Paddington heard a noise behind her.

ÜBUNG 30 !

Übung 30: Übersetzen Sie!

1. I have one particular station in mind.

2. She did it out of friendship, not for money.

3. He made Elvira's acquaintance in London last year.

4. The detective shook his head.

5. I would prefer it, if you stayed home.

6. Take care of yourself.

7. Miss Paddington smiles to herself.

8. The inspector stammers often.

The housekeeper spun around startled.
A strange man stood in the door to the living room. His clothes looked as if they had come from the Salvation Army. His whiskey breath was even stronger than the smell of frying bacon in the pan.
"What's for supper, baby?" the stranger asked and leaned against the door frame.
Miss Paddington gulped and reached for the frying pan.

Übung 31: Welches Wort ist richtig? Unterstreichen Sie es!

ÜBUNG 31 !

The frying pan in her hand, Miss Paddington ran towards the (1.) intruder/guest.
"Just wait, you crook!" cried the (2.) frightened/resolute housekeeper, swinging the pan like a (3.) baseball bat/flower.
The strange man raised his hands in (4.) fear/happiness.
"Miss Paddington, don't …!" he cried.
The old lady stopped. The voice was more than (5.) unknown/familiar. Then she gave the intruder a closer look.
Of course, his clothes were unacceptable and the whiskey breath (6.) unbearable/delightful, but the figure in the (7.) doorway/window could be none other than …

"Inspector Hudson? W-what in the hell is with this silly disguise? How could you frighten me so?" gasped Miss Paddington.
James Hudson took a step forward and put his hand on the angry housekeeper's shoulder.
"I'm sorry if I frightened you, Miss Paddington. I was trying out my disguise – but I didn't think it would be so convincing that even you wouldn't recognise me."

ÜBUNG 32

Übung 32: Setzen Sie das richtige Wort ein, um das Rätsel zu lösen.

1. bevorzugen ☐ _ _ _ _ _
2. fanatisch _ _ _ _ _ _ _ _ ☐
3. nachdenklich _ _ ☐ _ _ _ _ _ _ _
4. Handtasche _ ☐ _ _ _
5. Gespenst ☐ _ _ _ _
6. reichen, greifen nach _ _ _ _ ☐
7. Atemzug ☐ _ _ _ _ _
8. Speck _ _ _ ☐ _
9. Eindringling _ _ ☐ _ _ _ _ _
10. erschrecken _ _ _ _ _ ☐ _ _
11. erkennen _ _ _ ☐ _ _ _ _ _
12. Geruch _ ☐ _ _ _

Lösung: _ _ _ _ _ _ _ _ _ _ _ _

Miss Paddington glared at him and shook her head.
"James, you look absolutely awful. What is the disguise for?"

Übung 33: Bilden Sie sinnvolle Wörter aus dem Buchstabenchaos!

"Well," answered Hudson, "when I start looking for Jimmy Coltrane, I will have to go down into the underworld – in every 1. sesne _________ (Sinn) of the word. I'm 2. iaradf _________ (fürchten) that dear Jimmy isn't moving in the best social 3. lciscer _________ (Kreise) after his release from 4. srinop _________ (Gefängnis)."
"Most likely he is associating with thieves and scoundrels," grumbled Miss Paddington.
"Most likely. If I go into these circles as Inspector James Hudson and start asking 5. stupeananl ________ (unangenehm) questions, I would scare off my informants. But if Matches Marconi asks about his old prison buddy Jimmy Coltrane, no-one will be suspicious."
Miss Paddington 6. kolode _________ (blickte) at the Inspector inquisitively.
"Who is Matches Marconi?"
"Who else?" asked the inspector with a phony voice and put his hand on his 7. ethsc ________ (Brust), as 8. udts ________ (Staub) rose from the old suitcoat. "He's standing right in front of you."

Half an hour later, the inspector sat in a tube that brought him directly to the Holborn station. Miss Paddington had insisted that he eat a hearty meal before his undercover operation. In the meantime, the evening had already advanced and only a few commuters shared the compartment with Hudson.

The cheap whisky, which the inspector had drank, did its job – the other passengers looked at Hudson with disgust and moved as far away from him as possible. His disguise was working.

The train came to a halt with a jolt and the inspector lurched out of the car, during which he shoved another passenger. However, after a look from 'Matches Marconi' the passenger did not dare to complain.

Hudson was so into his role that he jumped in fright as an underground police officer stared searchingly at him. With quick steps, the inspector climbed the steps and had reached the construction site a minute later.

! ÜBUNG 34

Übung 34: Welches Wort ist das „schwarze Schaf"?

1. robbery, return, theft, steal ________
2. insignificant, minor, important, trivial ________
3. incompetent, talented, gifted, skilled ________
4. yellowed, old, fresh, faded ________
5. sole, exclusive, one, multiple ________
6. uninterested, mesmerised, entranced, hypnotised ________
7. precious, worthless, valuable, expensive ________
8. linked, interconnected, joined, independent ________

9. bachelor, husband, single, unmarried ______

10. supper, breakfast, evening meal, dinner ______

The skeleton of the imposing office building stretched sinisterly into the night sky. The full moon bathed the steel girders in silvery light. During the day, there was bustle and noise here, but in the moonlight, the construction site lay quiet and empty.
The inspector looked around.

Übung 35: Finden Sie die englische Übersetzung!
(1. Zaun 2. Baustelle 3. überzeugen 4. Durchsuchungsbefehl 5. Werkzeuge 6. Rohbau)

Good. No-one was around, and the street was empty. With deft movements, the inspector climbed over the wooden fence separating the construction site from the street. As he sprung down, Hudson hoped that the construction site wasn't patrolled by a security company. It would be difficult to convince the night watchman that an inspector from Scotland Yard was hidden under Matches Marconi's torn clothing – and Hudson didn't have a search warrant for the construction site.
Whichever way one looked at it, he was an illegal intruder on private property. However, without concrete evidence, it would have taken days, if not weeks, to receive a search warrant for this site.
Hudson pulled a flashlight out of his pocket and began to look around. He picked his way carefully between broken machines and piles of sand. Dozens of construction workers were here during the day. A gang of thieves with digging tools would hardly be noticed. After a few minutes, Hudson found what he was looking for:

20 metres from the skeleton was a small chute that led directly underground.

Around the entrance, one could recognise the remains of the old underground station – Hudson climbed in carefully. After a few minutes, he arrived at a wooden door.
"Entry prohibited. Danger. Collapse Hazard!" warned the sign. There was no doubt that these were the remains of the abandoned underground station. Hudson pulled a skeleton key out of his pocket and picked at the rusty lock. A few seconds later, the door opened with a click.

! ÜBUNG 36

Übung 36: Setzen Sie die passiven Sätze ins Aktiv!

1. The lop-sided steps were climbed by the inspector.

___

2. The steel girders were bathed in light by the moon.

___

3. The night watchman was not convinced by Hudson.

___

4. The property was entered by the intruder.

___

5. The construction site was patrolled by a security company.

___

6. A search warrant was issued by the judge.

---

7. The machines were used by nobody.

---

8. The station was shone on by the flashlight.

Hudson carefully pushed open the door and shone his flashlight in the darkness. A dusty set of stone steps led further into the depths. Damp and mould had made the steps slippery and the inspector had to carefully grope his way down. His steps echoed eerily in the dark. After a few minutes, he reached level ground.

Übung 37: Welches Wort bedeutet das Gegenteil?

1. careful
   a) ☐ cautious
   b) ☐ watchful
   c) ☐ reckless

2. abandoned
   a) ☐ full
   b) ☐ empty
   c) ☐ uninhabited

3. prohibited
   a) ☐ illegal
   b) ☐ allowed
   c) ☐ forbidden

4. hidden
   a) ☐ open
   b) ☐ secret
   c) ☐ unseen

5. moist
   a) ☐ damp
   b) ☐ wet
   c) ☐ dry

The inspector shone his flashlight until it caught a sign on the wall. 'British Museum' was written in weathered letters.
Hudson was actually standing on the platform of a station that had been abandoned a hundred years ago. The light beam was reflected on the tiled walls and bathed the station in a surreal glow. All of a sudden, the floor shook and a droning rattle filled the chute. A moist gust brushed the inspector's face.
He needed a few moments to realise what was going on. A regular tube was rattling through the central line that must run near here. There were connections between the old and new tunnels.

ÜBUNG 38 !

Übung 38: Bilden Sie aus dem Adjektiv ein Adverb!

1. social ____________________
2. suspicious ____________________
3. good ____________________
4. hearty ____________________

5. sinister ____________________

6. illegal ____________________

7. careful ____________________

8. rusty ____________________

9. actual ____________________

10. regular ____________________

The typical draught from a tube passing by could be felt in the abandoned tunnel. It's sure eerie here, thought Hudson. No wonder people called these stations 'ghost stations'. He wouldn't have been surprised if there were actually ghosts down here.

In truth, there were many legends about the souls of dead passengers, who were desperately looking for an exit.

At that moment, a shrill sound came from behind the inspector. Hudson wheeled around.

A shadowy figure rushed towards the inspector. Its mouth was opened in an angry scream and it glowed ghostly in the darkness.

Übung 39: Wie heißt das Verb auf Englisch?

ÜBUNG 39 !

1. strecken ____________________

2. sich schnell umdrehen ____________________

3. glühen/leuchten ____________________

4. irreführen ____________________

5. spiegeln ____________________

6. rasen ____________________

Elvira Elliot looked at her watch for the twentieth time. It was late and she had been sitting and waiting for over an hour in the elegant hotel bar. In the meantime, she would have been able to hum along with the melodies played by the pianist in the corner, if she had wanted to. But Elvira was tired. After she had left the inspector, she had been on telephone for hours trying to take advantage of her connections.

After a dozen calls to friends and colleagues in the insurance branch, she had been able to put together a list of all the art collectors, who had recently gone on a shopping spree in London.

Übung 40: Welche Wörter haben dieselbe Bedeutung?

1. tired	☐ competitor
2. melody	☐ lately
3. colleagues	☐ asset
4. recently	☐ rich
5. painting	☐ tune
6. investment	☐ co-workers
7. wealthy	☐ picture
8. rival	☐ sleepy
9. interested	☐ curious

It was unbelievable how much money people would spend on an old painting. At the same time, these artworks were solid investments which could be hung on the wall to show off.

No wonder, thought Elvira, that many rich Americans were in London in order to shower themselves with art from old England. And at this moment, Elvira was waiting for such an American – Bill B. Bixby, an oil tycoon from Texas.

Übung 41: Bringen Sie die Wörter in die richtige Reihenfolge!

1. spend art money a lot of People on

2. wait had to time a long Elvira

3. dealers She art many called

4. Picasso doesn't Hudson like

5. he saw Hudson thought ghost a

6. was scream A heard

7. London shop Many in collectors

An old friend, who worked for a rival insurance agency and owed Elvira a favour, had told her about how Mr Bixby was buying up portraits of old aristocrats like crazy.
Elvira was interested immediately as she thought about the relatively worthless third painting that was stolen. After a few more calls, Elvira had managed to actually set up an appointment with Mr Bixby.
Maybe he knew something about the missing painting. If he would only show.

ÜBUNG 42 !

Übung 42: Unterstreichen Sie die Wörter im Text mit denselben Bedeutungen!
(another time, found, yelled, lovely, thankful, truthful, dreadful)

Elvira was looking at her watch again, as a broad-shouldered man in a colourfully patterned suit entered the bar. Instead of a regular tie, two leather strings swung out of his collar bound together by a silver steer's head. Definitely a Texan.
The man looked around the bar and discovered Elvira, who was waving at him. Seconds later, he had crossed the bar with big steps. Before Elvira could say anything, the Texan was shaking her hand.
"You must be Miss Elliot," he shouted. "My name is Bixby. Bill B. Bixby from beautiful Austin, Texas."
"Without a doubt," smiled Elvira, "I'm grateful that you had time to meet me on such short notice."
"Now or never, honey. My plane leaves for Texas tomorrow morning. To be honest, I'm happy to be going home to sunny Texas. London in the autumn is terrible."

"I won't take much of your time, Mr Bixby," answered Elvira, "I wanted to ask if you knew something about a painting."
Mr Bixby waved to a waitress.
"Hey, honey," he shouted across the room, "the young lady and I will have Kentucky whiskeys!"
Elvira tried to protest, but the Texan did not notice.
"Uhhm, no thank you, Mr Bixby. What I wanted to say was … this painting …"
The Texan laid his big, fleshy hand on Elvira's wrist.
"I'm sorry lady. I admire your sense of business, but I've already insured my paintings."
Elvira shook her head.

"Mr Bixby, you have the wrong idea. I don't want to sell you an insurance policy. I'm afraid that the painting you bought here in London could have been stolen."

Übung 43: Welche Übersetzung gibt die Bedeutung des englischen Satzes wieder?

1. If he would only show.
   a) ☐ Wenn er nur zeigen würde.
   b) ☐ Wenn er nur auftauchen würde.
   c) ☐ Wenn er nur darstellen würde.

2. London in the autumn is terrible.
   a) ☐ London im Sommer ist schrecklich
   b) ☐ London im Herbst ist beängstigend.
   c) ☐ London im Herbst ist schrecklich.

3. Definitely a Texan.
   a) ☐ Eindeutig ein Texaner.
   b) ☐ Vielleicht ein Texaner.
   c) ☐ Auf keinen Fall ein Texaner.

4. I won't take much of your time.
   a) ☐ Ich brauche viel Ihrer Zeit.
   b) ☐ Ich werde nicht viel Ihrer Zeit in Anspruch nehmen.
   c) ☐ Ich werde Ihre Zeit nicht brauchen.

5. I admire your business sense.
   a) ☐ Ich verachte Ihren Geschäftssinn.
   b) ☐ Ich bewundere Ihren Geschäftspartner.
   c) ☐ Ich bewundere Ihren Geschäftssinn.

Bixby looked at Elvira with astonishment.
"Stolen! What do you mean?"
"Well, I heard that you bought a large number of aristocrat portraits in the past few weeks."
"That's true," nodded Bixby, as he interrupted Elvira. "Do you know, I bought a small country seat in the North of England. I am having it taken apart brick by brick and having it rebuilt on my ranch in Texas. I needed a few paintings for the interior."
Elvira almost fainted when she thought about how much it must cost to tear down, transport and rebuild an entire house, probably in the middle of a cow pasture.

ÜBUNG 44 !

Übung 44: Was wird beschrieben?

1. A place to live, usually in the United States or Australia, where there are often horses, cows and sheep. ______
2. Many of these are used to build houses. ______
3. The season of the year where the leaves change colour. ______
4. Money paid to protect an object, such as a painting or your life. ______
5. Feeling sorry because someone else has problems. ______
6. An area away from the city where fewer people live. ______
7. A woman who serves you in a restaurant. ______

"Oh really," continued Elvira, "and as chance would have it, yesterday night the portrait of a certain Lord Ploughbottom was stolen from a gallery and it is possible that the thieves could have offered it to you."

Mr Bixby went pale.

"What was his name?"

"Lord Ploughbottom. The painting is from the late 17th century."

"Oh dear," murmured Bixby, "that's impossible. The picture was stolen, you said?"

"Yesterday night, from the Blighton-Gallery – together with two more valuable paintings from …"

"Picasso and Monet?"

For a moment, Elvira was surprised that the Texan knew these artists names. Then she nodded.

"Those crooks were fast," Bixby remarked, after regaining his composure. "This afternoon, a guy came to me and offered me those exact paintings. His name was Coltrane, or …"

"Coltrane?" cried Elvira.

Übung 45: Gibt der Satz den Sachverhalt richtig wieder? Markieren Sie: richtig ✓ falsch –

ÜBUNG 45 !

1. Elvira didn't have to wait long at the hotel bar.
2. Mr Bixby was from Houston.
3. Mr Bixby's plane was leaving the next day.
4. Mr Bixby ordered gin for himself and Elvira.
5. Mr Bixby thought that Elvira was trying to sell him insurance.
6. Mr Bixby is transporting the country house he bought to Texas.
7. Mr Bixby lives in an apartment.

8. Mr Bixby was offered all three stolen paintings.
9. Mr Bixby is a great admirer of Picasso and Monet.
10. Mr Bixby said that Jimmy Coltrane visited him that afternoon.

Bixby nodded.
"That's him. He told me that he had to sell off his collection due to financial troubles. I didn't want the Picasso and the Monet. I don't like pictures where I can't make anything out. But I bought the lord immediately. It fits perfectly in my collection."
Elvira was so excited, that she even took a sip from the whiskey glass.

ÜBUNG 46 !

Übung 46: Bilden Sie Wörter aus dem Buchstabenchaos!

"Do you still have the painting here?" she gasped.

Bixby 1. dndedo ______________ (nickte).

"Of 2. ucoser ________________ (natürlich). And if it was really 3. lsonet ______________ (geklaut), I will 4. veale ______________ (zurücklassen) it with you. It wasn't very 5. ixesnevpe ________________ (teuer) anyway. Could you take it to the police for me tomorrow? I'm afraid I would 6. sims ____________________ (verpassen) my 7. glifth ______________ (Flug) if I did it myself."

Elvira nodded vigorously.
"Of course."
Bixby emptied his glass in one gulp and stood up.

"Can you wait here for a moment. I will go get the painting from my room."
Elvira watched the Texan from behind and rejoiced. Hudson would stare when she presented him the stolen painting.
Elvira couldn't see Bill Bixby get in the elevator with an evil smile on his face.

Übung 47: Setzen Sie die richtige Präposition ein!

1. Miss Paddington looked ________ her watch.
2. Sir Reginald waved ________ the forensics team.
3. Elvira is ________ Manchester.
4. Hudson was ready to go ________ short notice.
5. Many paintings were stolen ________ the past few weeks.
6. Bixby has many horses ________ his ranch.
7. Hudson offered a cigarette ________ Elvira.
8. The gallery was closed due ________ the thefts.
9. He couldn't make anything ________ in the dark.
10. Hudson left his coat ________ Miss Paddington.

At the same moment the ghostly figure rushed towards Hudson. Instinctively, Hudson ducked. He felt something brush against his cheek and float away. The inspector rolled on the dusty ground, jumped up and looked around. The 'ghost' had disappeared – if it really *had* been a ghost that had attacked him.

Hudson brushed the dust off his jacket. The scream echoed eerily in the tunnel along with the drone of the tube. Then it was quiet. Hudson concentrated on his breathing and tried to regulate his pulse. Normally the inspector didn't believe in ghosts and supernatural apparitions, but the sudden spook had scared him.
But, as was the case whenever he was involved with supposedly unexplainable circumstances, his mind was already racing to find a logical explanation.
The appearance of the ghost was almost simultaneous with the passing of the tube. This was no coincidence. Hudson glanced at his watch. In a few moments, the train from the opposite direction should be passing.

ÜBUNG 48 !

Übung 48: Das englische Wort hat verschiedene Übersetzungsmöglichkeiten. Welche?

1. kind ____________ ____________
2. ball ____________ ____________
3. desert ____________ ____________
4. race ____________ ____________
5. mine ____________ ____________
6. like ____________ ____________
7. compliment ____________ ____________

A muffled rattling announced the train's approach and became louder the nearer it came.

All of a sudden, the shrill scream was heard again. A few seconds later, the ghostly figure appeared in exactly the same spot as before.

But this time, the inspector was prepared. Instead of throwing himself to the ground, he jumped in front of the 'ghost' and grabbed it.

His hands felt a thin material, as he heard a ripping noise. The 'ghost' stopped immediately and fell to the ground in front of him. In his hand, the inspector held a piece of fabric that glowed in the dark.

Hudson smiled as he picked up the rest of the painted sheet. Someone had painted the outline of a horrible ghost with glow paint. Above, the distorted face was a loop.

Hudson shone his flashlight at the ceiling. If one knew what to look for, one could find a thin rope stretched from one end of the tunnel to the other.

Übung 49: Bilden Sie sinnvolle Sätze!

1. explanation There a must logical be

2. in Miss Paddington ghosts believes

3. train the of The heard rattle again was

4. dark Her in glowed the eyes

____

5. the Did ghost see anyone?

____

6. by Elvira disguise Hudson's frightened was

____

7. Hudson coming he as saw Elvira smiled

____

8. the waited Elvira questions and answers for asked

____

9. smiling is Mr Bixby Why?

____

10. waitress He a whiskey for the asked

____

Undoubtedly, the 'ghost' and the rope were part of a clever mechanism that was released by the draught from the passing trains.

An effective method for keeping unwanted visitors away or for scaring homeless people who wandered into the tunnel by accident. Basically, the mechanical ghost was nothing more than a refined version of a scarecrow.

Only people who had something to protect would put up a scarecrow. Or people who had something to hide.

Übung 50: Beantworten Sie die Fragen zum Text!

1. What legends were connected with the 'ghost stations'?

2. Why did Hudson hope that no-one patrolled the construction site?

3. Why did Hudson disguise himself as Matches Marconi?

4. What did Hudson first think he saw in the tunnel?

5. What was the connection between the 'ghost' and the subway?

Hudson shone his flashlight further around the tunnel. Now that he had got used to the darkness and exorcised the spook from the 'ghost station', he began to enjoy his underground expedition. It was a trip into the past. The flashlight's beam caught a yellowed newspaper from 1933.

"Paul Adrien Maurice Dirac and Erwin Schrödinger share the Nobel Prize for their new theory of the atom," announced the headlines on the front page. Next to the paper, lay an old ticket, on which was printed a price which seemed extremely low by today's standards.

The inspector allowed himself a nostalgic smile. Then, he discovered something in the corner of the station, under a rotting bench, which was much more interesting. Hudson knelt in front of the bench and pulled out a belt which held various tools and a dust mask. The belt was worn, but definitely not 70 years old. It must belong to the thieves, who had entered the tunnel system from this station.

In his searching fever, the inspector searched the numerous small pockets and straps. At last, something small and square fell out: a matchbook. The inspector aimed his flashlight beam at it.

'King's Head Inn' was written on the front.

Übung 51: Welches Wort hat die gegenteilige Bedeutung?

1.	quiet	☐ whisper
2.	supernatural	☐ reveal
3.	yell	☐ drop
4.	float	☐ irrational
5.	appear	☐ welcome
6.	logical	☐ normal
7.	coincidental	☐ sink
8.	lift	☐ vanish
9.	effective	☐ dislike
10.	unwanted	☐ noisy
11.	hide	☐ new
12.	enjoy	☐ useless
13.	worn	☐ planned

Inspector Hudson smiled again. He knew the pub, a nasty hole on the edge of town, a meeting point for crooks and their disreputable companions. Exactly the right place for Matches Marconi to wait for an old friend.

Übung 52: Fügen Sie die richtige Präposition ein!

Inspector Hudson, disguised 1. _________ Matches Marconi, had to change trains three times to get 2. ___________ the abandoned street where the 'King's Head Inn' was hidden.

Of course he could have taken a cab, but he doubted that any cab driver would have been willing to take someone like Marconi as a passenger. Furthermore, it wouldn't have made his disguise very convincing. 3. __________ the meantime, it was 4. ___________ midnight. According to the legal closing times, the bar should have shut a long time ago.

However, the owners and guests of the 'King's Head' did not seem to pay attention 5. _______ the regulations. Why should they obey the law by night, when they broke it 6. ___________ the daytime? A policeman seldom wandered into this run-down area, thought Hudson. He also doubted that the owner of the 'King's Head' even had a liquor license to lose.

Hudson was hardly ten paces 7. _________ from the bar, when the door was pushed open 8. _________ inside.

Two powerful, broad-shouldered men had grabbed a guest by the collar and threw him onto the street. Laughter emanated from the inside as the door shut again.

The drunk babbled something and reached into the pocket of his decrepit trousers.

ÜBUNG 53

Übung 53: Bilden Sie sinnvolle Wörter aus dem Buchstabenchaos!

1. EUBT (U-Bahn) ________________
2. SPUEL (Herzschlag) ________________
3. OREP (Seil) ________________
4. HDARGTU (Luftzug) ________________
5. WCRREASCO (Vogelscheuche) ________________
6. BPU (Kneipe) ________________
7. DIDHNE (versteckt) ________________
8. ENOWR (Inhaber) ________________
9. HIDNTIGM (Mitternacht) ________________
10. SIEECNL (Genehmigung) ________________

He pulled out a bundle of banknotes and a gold watch – and all of a sudden, he was sober.
Smiling and sure-footed, he walked away, counting the banknotes.
"Did you make a good catch?" asked the inspector.
Obviously the man was only pretending to be drunk, in order to bump into the other guests and pick their pockets. So much for honour among thieves.
The pickpocket startled and stared at the inspector, then ran off.
Hudson wrinkled his forehead as he thought. This was the perfect opportunity to win the trust of the men at the 'King's Head'.

Without hesitating, he sprinted after the pickpocket. The pick-pocket was horrified when he saw Hudson behind him and ran even faster.

Übung 54: Welche Wörter gehören zusammen?

1. underground
   a) ☐ airport b) ☐ tunnel c) ☐ river

2. pickpocket
   a) ☐ money b) ☐ safe c) ☐ alarm

3. bar
   a) ☐ tea b) ☐ cake c) ☐ alcohol

4. frame
   a) ☐ sculpture b) ☐ picture c) ☐ record

5. ghost
   a) ☐ scream b) ☐ laugh c) ☐ smile

6. police
   a) ☐ education b) ☐ law c) ☐ money

7. bachelor
   a) ☐ husband b) ☐ single c) ☐ wife

Nevertheless, Hudson was able to catch him. Police work kept him in shape. The inspector tackled the fleeing man and both men hit the ground hard. Hudson stood up quickly and grabbed the thief by

his collar. The thief tried hard to escape Hudson's grip.
"Hey! What's the deal here? Let me go you bastard!" cried the man angrily.
But Hudson was already dragging him back to the pub.Without a word, Hudson kicked the door open.

ÜBUNG 55 !

Übung 55: Finden Sie die englische Übersetzung für die Wörter in Klammern! ***(ohrenbetäubend, Gespräch, schweigen, genannt, hinter, kahl, fettig, Kumpel)***

The noise in the pub was deafening – laughter, conversation and loud music. However, everyone silenced as Hudson, alias Matches Marconi, entered the pub.
The pickpocket went pale.
The owner behind the bar, a fat, bald man with a greasy apron, looked questioningly at 'Matches Marconi'.
"What are you doing, mate? We just threw that drunk out!"

"Maybe," growled the inspector in his 'Marconi' voice, "but your friend here picked your pockets before. Cough it up buddy!"
The pickpocket gulped. Hesitatingly, he reached into the pockets of his trousers and pulled out the bundle of banknotes and the gold watch and laid them on the sticky table.
"No way!" cried a burly man in a greasy suit. "My fake Rolex!"
The man rushed to the table and snatched up the watch while he stared at the banknotes with greedy eyes.
"My money!" cried a dozen men at the same time. All at once, they all pounced on the money.
A few seconds later, a fight broke out, much to the amusement of the other guests.

Übung 56: Wie heißt das Wort auf Englisch?

1. Fang ____________________________
2. Geldschein ____________________________
3. Taschendieb ____________________________
4. nüchtern ____________________________
5. runzeln ____________________________
6. Gelegenheit ____________________________
7. vortäuschen ____________________________
8. schleppen ____________________________

The fat bartender laughed and turned the music on again.

Hudson used the noise to whisper in the pickpocket's ear: "You should look for another job, buddy. Now get out, before it gets ugly here."

The pickpocket didn't wait. He disappeared out the door and into the darkness like a flash of lightning.

"Come on over, mate!" called the bartender. "You deserve a beer."

Hudson snapped his fingers.

"Nothing against that my friend," he replied and took the pint of beer.

The other guests toasted him. Twenty minutes later Matches Marconi had toasted with most of the guests.

"Time for phase 2," thought the inspector, as he wiped the foam from his lips.

"… and while the police were still surrounding the bank, I hopped into a taxi with the loot and drove home!"

Inspector Hudson had already been entertaining the dubious persons with made-up capers that he had carried out as the famous Matches Marconi.

! ÜBUNG 57

Übung 57: Wie heißt das Simple Past des Verbs?

1. reply ______________________
2. throw ______________________
3. win ______________________
4. grab ______________________
5. beseech ______________________
6. pay ______________________
7. doubt ______________________
8. shrink ______________________

During these stories, he secretly switched his full beer glass with his listeners' empty ones – he needed a clear head to carry out his plans.

The crooks at the bar listened attentively to his stories and regularly slapped him on the back. Matches Marconi was the star of the evening.

"It's time to get to the point," thought Hudson.

"Actually boys, the reason I came is that I'm looking for an old mate of mine, Jimmy Coltrane – have you guys heard of him?"

"Jimmy Coltrane?" asked a bearded man. "The mole?"

Übung 58: Übersetzen Sie den Satz ins Englische!

ÜBUNG 58 !

1. Der Wirt bietet Hudson ein Bier an.

---

2. Der Taschendieb tut nur so, als ob er betrunken wäre.

---

3. Die Diebe ignorieren die Gesetze.

---

4. Hudsons Atem roch nach Whiskey.

---

5. Er stellte sich als Matches Marconi vor.

"That's him," nodded Hudson. "We were together in jail. Nice guy, Jimmy. I lost track of him after my, eh, unexpected release. But I owe him some money – and Matches Marconi always pays his debts. Do you guys know anything about him?"

Inspector Hudson tried to make the question sound as casual as possible. At the same time, his eyes swept over the other men and noted their reactions.

Most of the guests shrugged their shoulders.

"Sorry Matches," said the bearded man. "All I know is that he spent some time in prison. Then I didn't hear from him any more. What about you guys?"

The other guests shook their heads.

But two men sitting at the bar exchanged dark glances. One of them wore a blindingly bright plaid shirt, while the face of the other one was etched with a narrow scar.
When the man in plaid motioned to the bartender to pay, Hudson glanced at the man's hands unnoticed by the others.

Übung 59: Setzen Sie die richtigen Wörter ein, um das Geheimwort zu entschlüsseln!

1. Fingernagel _ _ _ _ _ _ _ _ _ ☐
2. vorherrschend _ _ _ _ ☐ _ _ _ _ _ _
3. Einkommen _ _ _ ☐ _ _ _ _
4. Belohnung _ _ _ _ _ ☐
5. Obdachloser _ ☐ _ _ _ _ _ _
6. unbemerkt _ ☐ _ _ _ _ _ _ _

Lösung: _ _ _ _ _ _

The man's fingernails were circled with dirt. Either the man had bad hygiene, or he had recently been digging. Hudson guessed the latter, due to the suspicious way the men looked when he mentioned Jimmy Coltrane.
Both men seemed not to be able to leave the bar fast enough. The man with the scar reached into his trousers pockets and pulled a bundle of pound notes. Without waiting for change, he laid a big banknote on the bar, emptied his beer glass in one gulp and left the bar with his friend.
The inspector watched them go, then slapped the bearded man on the back.

"OK, boys, that's all for tonight. I'm leaving. It was nice meeting you all."
Hudson got up from his stool, shook a few hands and left the bar with quick steps.
The inspector took a deep breath in the fresh air. He would probably smell like smoke and old beer for the next week.
He looked around. The men were hurrying down the street. The inspector quietly followed them.

Übung 60: Ersetzen Sie das unterstrichene Wort durch das Gegenteil!

1. It was terrible to meet you. __________
2. The ghost in the underground tunnel was real. __________
3. The two men at the bar were trusting of Hudson. __________
4. Criminals obey the laws. __________
5. The men were strolling down the street. __________
6. Matches Marconi was disliked by the other guests. __________

The crooks constantly looked back suspiciously, but Hudson was a professional – every Scotland Yard cadet learned the essentials of good trailing.
The men crept further into a run-down industrial section on the very edge of London. After 45 minutes, they reached their destination.
Hudson hid deeper in the dark and watched them from a safe distance, as they took one last look around before disappearing

into the warehouse. Hudson counted to ten, then quickly moved towards the door the men had used. He was alone and unarmed. If he wanted to subdue the thieves, he would have to use the element of surprise.
He took one more deep breath before carefully opening the warehouse door and slipping inside.

! ÜBUNG 61

Übung 61: Setzen Sie die richtige Präposition ein!

The air was full of a mouldy smell. The inspector's eyes needed a few minutes to adjust 1. ___________ the darkness. Hudson crept 2. ______________ a few old crates and listened. He heard two voices arguing 3. ___________ a corner of the building.

"Do you think the guy was a cop?" asked one voice.

"Nope. He was way too scummy. Maybe he heard about our coup and wanted to get some of the money."

Hudson moved quietly towards the voices.

The men were standing in front of two paintings carelessly leaned 4. _______________ the wall. Although the inspector was no art expert, the pictures' details could not be mistaken: one of the paintings, undoubtedly the Picasso, showed a guitar that seemed to have been painted 5. _________ three different angles at the same time. The second painting was a wonderful combination of colours in elegantly applied brushstrokes. The picture was of a small houseboat, peacefully 6. __________ a river. It must be the Monet. The thief in plaid pointed to the paintings.

"What money?" he said scornfully. "7. ___________ now we only have the pathetic advance, that Jimmy Coltrane gave us. Ever 8. ___________ that, we haven't heard anything from him, and no one wants to buy these old things. They're too well-known and therefore too dangerous."

Hudson jumped out. The crooks jumped in horror.
"Crime doesn't pay," cried Hudson. "Inspector James Hudson from Scotland Yard. You're under arrest."
The man with the scar got over his surprise first.
"Oh yeah," he growled, "you and who else?"
Then he raised his fists and rushed at Hudson.
The inspector elegantly sidestepped him, and his attacker punched the air. Thrown off balance by his own offensive, he became an easy target. Hudson threw a punch and sent the man to the ground.

Übung 62: Wie lautet das Sprichwort auf Deutsch?

! ÜBUNG 62

1. Crime doesn't pay.

____

2. The early bird catches the worm.

____

3. It went like clockwork.

The second crook was more careful. Obviously, he wasn't in the mood for hand-to-hand combat with Hudson.
Instead, he pulled out a pistol from his belt. "I thought that something was funny with you," he shouted. "But it was a mistake to follow us here alone. It'll be your last mistake."
Hudson raised his hands. He had planned on this.
"Don't do anything stupid, man," he said calmly. At the same time, he carefully took a few steps backwards. Behind him was a wall of empty cardboard boxes.
The man with the scar raised the gun and slowly pulled the trigger, in order not to lose the weapon when it fired.

ÜBUNG 63 !

Übung 63: Wie heißt das Verb auf Englisch?

1. graben

2. leeren

3. verstecken

4. sich gewöhnen an

5. lehnen

6. brüllen

Even though it was clear that this was not the first time the crook had handled a weapon, the inspector knew what he was doing. He pretended to cower in fear until his heel touched the pile of boxes. Then he waited for the right moment.

“Say your prayers,” grinned the crook. Hudson shut his eyes.

“It’s too early for that,” was all he said and kicked one of the lowest boxes.

The boxes slid down in a cascade. The criminal instinctively raised his hand to protect his face.

Hudson had waited for this moment. He ignored the harmless boxes, rushed forward, and punched the man on the jaw.

Übung 64: Wählen Sie die richtige Antwort auf die Frage!

1. Where are you going?
   - a) ☐ I’m going to be a Scotland Yard inspector.
   - b) ☐ I’m going to the movies.
   - c) ☐ I’m going crazy.

2. What do you do for a living?
   - a) ☐ I’m an insurance agent.
   - b) ☐ I live at 221 Baker Street.
   - c) ☐ I do portraits in my spare time.

3. How do you know that?
   - a) ☐ I read it in the newspaper.
   - b) ☐ I like the Rolling Stones.
   - c) ☐ I was in Dublin last week.

4. What are you studying at Cambridge?
   a) ☐ I'm looking at this magazine.
   b) ☐ I'm studying economics.
   c) ☐ I'm studying the adverts for a job.

5. What are you doing at the weekend?
   a) ☐ I'm going to Spain for two weeks.
   b) ☐ I went to the British Museum.
   c) ☐ I'm going to clean my flat.

The man gave a moan of surprise as he fell among the boxes. Hudson rubbed his hand and looked around. In one corner of the warehouse he saw a table with tools and tape, which he used to bind the crooks' hands, before they regained consciousness.

Hudson surveyed his work with satisfaction, reached into his jacket pocket and pulled out his mobile phone. He dialled the number of the police.

Then he sat down on the boxes and admired the two precious paintings in front of him.

Maybe I should learn more about art, he thought, as sirens blared in the distance and announced the arrival of the first police car.

! ÜBUNG 65

Übung 65: Welche Person wird mit welchem Bereich assoziiert?

1. William Shakespeare	☐	science
2. Pablo Picasso	☐	politics
3. Albert Einstein	☐	art
4. Ingmar Bergman	☐	music
5. Tony Blair	☐	literature
6. W. A. Mozart	☐	cinema

7. Paul Bocuse ☐ charity
8. Sister Theresa ☐ nobility
9. Count Dracula ☐ cooking

A few minutes later Hudson was talking to the beat officer and had given a short testimony for the record. The crooks were in custody and the paintings would be returned to the gallery tomorrow.
In spite of this, Hudson still looked gloomy.
"Is something wrong, sir?" asked one of the officers. "You have every right to be satisfied. You caught two wanted criminals and rescued two invaluable paintings. Not a bad night's work, if you ask me."

Übung 66: Setzen Sie das richtige Wort ein!
(harmless, testimony, announce, protect, punched, dialled)

ÜBUNG 66 !

1. He wants to __________ his family from harm.

2. I'm sorry. I must have __________ the wrong number.

3. Don't be afraid of the dog. He's __________.

4. He got so mad at Matches, that he __________ him.

5. Hudson's __________ will be invaluable in court.

6. Elvira will __________ her discovery at tomorrow's meeting.

Hudson shrugged his shoulders.
"Maybe. But the ringleader is still free. The case isn't closed, until I have caught Jimmy Coltrane."
"Do you mean Jimmy the Mole?"

Hudson nodded in amazement.
"Do you know something I don't know?" he asked.
The officer shut his notebook.
"I think so, sir. Up until recently, I worked in the prison where old Jimmy was, until three months ago …"
"I didn't know that Jimmy was behind bars again. How did he get out? Was he released or did he escape?"
The officer shook his head.
"Neither, sir. Jimmy Coltrane died peacefully in his cell, three months ago."

! ÜBUNG 67

Übung 67: Welche Übersetzung stimmt? Kreuzen Sie an!

	a)		b)	
1. außer Sichtweite	a) ☐	out of sight	b) ☐	out of look
2. arbeitslos	a) ☐	out of labour	b) ☐	out of work
3. veraltet	a) ☐	out of date	b) ☐	out of up to date
4. außer Gefahr	a) ☐	out of pain	b) ☐	out of danger
5. nicht vorrätig	a) ☐	out of cellar	b) ☐	out of stock
6. atemlos	a) ☐	out of breath	b) ☐	out of air

Inspector Hudson sat at the kitchen table, freshly showered and shaved, and drank a cup of Earl Grey. He had slept poorly. He couldn't stop thinking about Jimmy Coltrane.
Coltrane had been dead for months – but the two tunnel thieves had worked with him – or thought they had.
The inspector had asked both criminals for a description of Coltrane. They corresponded exactly with the inspector's own memories of Jimmy the Mole.

Übung 68: Setzen Sie das richtige Verb in der korrekten Form ein!

The whole thing was completely strange. Who was (1. vorgeben) __________ to be Jimmy Coltrane, and why?

Miss Paddington (2. gießen) _________ herself another cup of tea and shook her head.

"Old Jimmy is dead? That's too bad. He was a total lunk, but I liked him."

Hudson nodded.

"I know Miss Paddington. Jimmy was a crook, but an old school criminal. He never would (3. angreifen) ______________ anyone with a weapon – like the ones I (4. fangen) _______________ yesterday in the warehouse. The real Jimmy never would (5. sich verbünden) ____________________ with such creatures."

Hudson and Miss Paddington looked up as the doorbell rang.

It was Elvira Elliot. She (6. anrufen) ____________________ early because she wanted to stop by and show the inspector something.

"I'll get it," said the inspector and got up to open the door for the young lady.

"Good morning, James," Elvira beamed as Hudson opened the door. She had a large, flat package in her hand, which had been carefully wrapped in brown packing paper.

"James, listen … you'll never guess what I have here!"

"Mmmh … let me try anyway. The portrait of Lord Ploughbottom?" Elvira looked at the inspector for a moment with disappointment. Then she smilingly shook her head. "How did you know, James?"
"Come in first, Elvira. Yesterday I was also out and about in the cause of art and was able to take back the precious Monet and Picasso."

Übung 69: Haben die Wörter dieselbe Bedeutung? Markieren Sie: richtig ✓ falsch –

1. conscious/aware
2. admire/hate
3. precious/priceless
4. satisfied/content
5. rescue/lose
6. amazement/astonishment
7. peaceful/turbulent
8. dead/deceased
9. guess/estimate
10. disappointment/joy

"Really?" gasped Elvira. "How did you manage that?"
The inspector led Elvira into the kitchen, where Miss Paddington was already waiting with a cup of tea. Hudson told her about his little adventure as Matches Marconi. In return, Elvira recounted how Bill B. Bixby voluntarily turned over the stolen Ploughbottom painting to her.
"Thankfully I didn't have to argue with the guy," concluded Elvira. "He was a totally crude man. *Autumn in London is horrible.*" Elvira did her best to imitate the broad Texas accent.

Miss Paddington laughed, but Hudson stared at Elvira with astonishment.
“What did you say?” he asked Elvira with a raised eyebrow.
“What? I was just trying to imitate Mr Bixby’s accent. You know, Texans always talk as if they had a fist full of chewing gum in their mouths. They probably do.”
“No, no,” answered the inspector seriously. “Did he really say London in *autumn*?”

Übung 70: Welche Übersetzung stimmt?

1. Ich mache die Tür auf.
   a) ☐ I opened the door.
   b) ☐ I have opened the door.
   c) ☐ I’ll open the door.

2. Wie hast du das gemacht?
   a) ☐ How did you do it?
   b) ☐ How will you do it?
   c) ☐ How can you do it?

3. Er spricht, als ob er Kaugummi im Mund hätte.
   a) ☐ He talks when he has chewing gum in his mouth.
   b) ☐ He talks like he has chewing gum in his mouth.
   c) ☐ He talks with chewing gum in his mouth.

4. He gave her the painting back.
   a) ☐ Er kann ihr das Gemälde nicht zurückgeben.
   b) ☐ Er wird ihr das Gemälde zurückgeben.
   c) ☐ Er gab ihr das Gemälde zurück.

Elvira was perplexed.
"Yes, James. Why? What's so unusual about that?"
"Nothing at first," said Hudson thoughtfully, "but a real American, especially a Texan, would never use the word 'autumn'".
Elvira looked at Hudson with wide eyes.
"You're right, James. Americans usually say 'fall'. Just like they say elevator instead of lift."

ÜBUNG 71 !

Übung 71: Bilden Sie sinnvolle Wörter aus dem Buchstabenchaos!

"You're right. I'm afraid your genuine Texan was 1. herytiengv __________ (alles) but genuine. It was probably an Englishman who was pretending to be a Texan."

"And made a tiny 2. kimesta ______________ (Fehler)," continued Elvira. "But why? Why did he pretend to be an 3. cmenrAia __________ (amerikanischer) businessman?"

Hudson 4. otko ____________ (nahm) another 5. psi ____________ (Schluck) of tea. Yes, why? That was the 6. amni ______________ (Haupt-) question. 7. yMbae ______________ (vielleicht) the man suspected that the painting was stolen and bought the painting from the thieves under an assumed identity.

Normally, James Hudson would have been satisfied with the fact that all three paintings were recovered – but there was this Jimmy Coltrane problem.

In this case, someone else had obviously pretended to be Coltrane – for whatever reason. It could hardly be a coincidence – quite the opposite. Hudson turned pale at his own conclusion.

Übung 72: Welches Wort ist das „schwarze Schaf"?

ÜBUNG 72 !

1. imitate, insult, copy, mimic ______
2. seriously, earnestly, jokingly, gravely ______
3. really, actually, honestly, laughingly ______
4. understanding, perplexed, puzzled, confused ______
5. usually, never, generally, commonly ______
6. safety, shelter, protection, harm ______
7. everyday, unusual, surprising, extraordinary ______
8. gaze, ignore, stare, watch ______

After a long pause he said: "I suspect that your Mr Bixby and my Jimmy Coltrane imitator are the same person."

"Really?" Elvira looked at Hudson doubtfully. "He must be a master of disguises."

Hudson nodded.

"I'm afraid you're right. Does the name 'The Phantom' mean anything to you?"

Elvira gasped.

"The Phantom? Seriously, James. You don't think that this legend really exists?"

"The Phantom?" chimed in Miss Paddington.

Hudson wanted to start explaining but Elvira was first.
"For years, a rumour has been circulating about a faceless master criminal, who was responsible for a number of unsolved cases. No one has ever seen his face or knows who he is. He is a sort of modern Fu Man Chu."

Übung 73: Bilden Sie sinnvolle Sätze!

1. painting lied He the about

___

2. be did he businessman to pretend Why a?

___

3. master is disguise a of He

___

4. Mr Mr person and Coltrane are Bixby same the

___

5. not was satisfied still Hudson

___

6. of Have the heard Phantom you?

___

7. I face never his have seen

___

"That's spooky," rejoined Miss Paddington. She was an avid reader of detective novels and could hardly conceal her excitement.
"I personally think this Phantom is just a legend. A ghost story that the police use when they can't solve a case. Sorry, James."
"It's OK, Elvira. But the fact is, that is exactly what you are supposed to think. Scotland Yard has been hunting the Phantom for years, but he has eluded us so far. The officials prefer the public not to believe in this criminal's existence. It would just make them afraid, since any citizen could be the Phantom. Who can one trust anymore?"
"You mean the Phantom really exists, and I was sitting at the same table with him? That's unbelievable!" cried Elvira.

Übung 74: Wie heißt das Wort auf Deutsch?

ÜBUNG 74 !

1. rumour	☐	gierig
2. circulation	☐	Gegenteil
3. responsible	☐	blass
4. doubtful	☐	Gerücht
5. avid	☐	Grund
6. pale	☐	verantwortlich
7. safety	☐	zweifelnd
8. reason	☐	Umlauf
9. opposite	☐	Sicherheit

"But true," nodded Hudson sadly. Then he stared sternly at Elvira and Miss Paddington, "I insist that this information remain confidential."
Both women nodded.

"Of course," said Elvira. "But why did the Phantom pretend to be Coltrane and Bixby? And why did he only keep the worthless painting? And why was he so willing to give it back?"
"I've been asking myself the same question," answered Hudson. "I think the Phantom wanted to play it safe. He disguised himself as Coltrane to make sure that the hired thieves didn't make off with the loot. He probably acted like the Texan to foil the police. Think about it. Two of the three criminals have been caught, the paintings returned … Scotland Yard would have probably had an intern finish clearing up the background information and everyone would have forgotten about the botched robbery in a few weeks."

ÜBUNG 75 !

Übung 75: Setzen Sie das richtige Wort ein!

Elvira nodded. "But why did he (1. behalten) ____________ the worthless painting at first – and then (2. zurückgeben) ________ it to me without hesitating?"

Hudson rubbed his (3. Kinn) __________ thoughtfully.

"I think that the Phantom only (4. stahl) __________ the Picasso and the Monet to divert (5. Aufmerksamkeit) ____________ from his real intention …"

Hudson pointed to the portrait, that was still in its (6. Packpapier) ________________.

"The (7. Tatsache) ______________ that he readily returned the painting indicates it was important for him at some point, but not any (8. mehr) __________."

Miss Paddington shook her head. "What do you mean?"

"I don't know," replied the inspector and reached for the package. "Let's take a closer look at the painting."

Hudson began to carefully (9. auspacken) _________ the painting. An old, middling portrait in oils appeared. Lord Ploughbottom (10. lächelte) __________ at the observer and held the two dice in his hand.

Hudson and Elvira recognized the painting from the gallery's catalogue.
The three examined the painting from top to bottom, but it contained no surprises, until Hudson turned the painting around …
"Aha," he cried triumphantly, "we've got it!"

Übung 76: Beantworten Sie die Fragen zum Text!

ÜBUNG 76 !

1. Why did Inspector Hudson sleep badly?

____

2. What was the real Jimmy Coltrane like?

____

3. How did Hudson realize that Bill Bixby was actually an Englishman?

____

4. Why did Scotland Yard tell the public that the Phantom doesn't exist?

____

5. What is depicted on the portrait?

____

Elvira Elliot and Miss Paddington stared at the back of the painting. The canvas had turned yellow with age, but on the lower right corner, there was a white rectangle.
"Very interesting," murmured Hudson. "Obviously someone recently hid something here. Based on the size and the shape, I would guess a piece of paper or an envelope."

ÜBUNG 77

Übung 77: Setzen Sie die richtige Präposition ein!

"So that was what the Phantom was really 1. _________," Elvira said. "He wasn't interested 2. _________ the painting at all."
Hudson nodded.
"It seems that way. But this realisation doesn't help us much, as long as we don't know what was in the letter. It could be anything, 3. _________ a treasure map to the combination for a safe. We can

only assume that the information is highly valuable, otherwise the Phantom wouldn't have taken the trouble to obtain it."

"And we know," continued Elvira, "that the paper must have been in the frame 4. ____________ a while, since the canvas is white where the paper was."

"Exactly, Elvira," nodded Hudson. "Elvira, can you find out 5. ____________ where Mr Blighton obtained the portrait of Lord Ploughbottom? I would guess that it came from an old family collection, probably from the lord's descendants."

Elvira nodded 6. __________ energy.

"No problem, James. A few telephone calls should do the trick. I will call from the office. Otherwise, people may get suspicious when they see a private number 7. ____________ their telephone display."

Elvira took another quick sip of her tea and got up.

"If you don't mind, James, I will take the picture with me and will make sure that Mr Blighton gets it back as soon as possible."

Hudson nodded.

"Go ahead. I am going to the Yard to look over all available files on the Phantom. I'm afraid, however, that there won't be much information."

Hudson and Elvira said goodbye to Miss Paddington and promised to keep her posted on the progress of the investigation. Then they left the house, got into their cars, and drove away.

Neither of them noticed the outlandishly dressed young man passing by the inspector's house wearing a walkman.
And neither of them would have thought that a sophisticated microphone was hidden in the walkman.
The Phantom smiled. He had heard enough. Now it was time to act.

ÜBUNG 78

Übung 78: Übersetzen Sie die Redewendungen!

1. keep somebody posted

____

2. come like a bolt out of the blue

____

3. pull a dirty trick on someone

____

4. double-cross someone

____

5. be on the fiddle

____

Inspector Hudson sat at the desk of his tiny office and flipped through the disappointingly thin file that contained all the information about the mysterious Phantom.
It was true that the Phantom was suspected of a connection to a number of crimes.

And all of these crimes had one thing in common – the Phantom had committed the crime with the help of a perfect disguise and disappeared with his loot without a trace …
In Glasgow, a director of a bank walked into his safe room and had a pleasant conversation with the security guard. Then he strolled out with a million pounds. That same evening, the real director of the bank was found tied up in his apartment.

Übung 79: Bilden Sie synonyme Paare!

ÜBUNG 79

1. tiny	☐	aid
2. disappointingly	☐	nice
3. connection	☐	small
4. sense	☐	vanish
5. help	☐	tied
6. disappear	☐	association
7. bound	☐	meaning
8. pleasant	☐	flat
9. apartment	☐	frustratingly

The European continent was also not safe from the Phantom's greedy clutches. In Germany, the test driver of a top secret automobile prototype simply drove off the test course onto a nearby motorway. The real test driver was found well bound in a bathroom. The prototype's producers assume that the Phantom sold the prototype and its improvements in Asia for millions, where a cheap copy was produced.
One would think that such a successful criminal would retire with his money. But, if the Phantom was willing to go to such lengths

to get his hands on a piece of paper, then it must be something big. This knowledge made the inspector's stomach churn nervously.

ÜBUNG 80 !

Übung 80: Unterstreichen Sie das richtige Wort!

Elvira Elliot (1.) sped/drove slowly through the rolling hills.
She actually had only needed two telephone calls to find the (2.) future/previous (3.) mother/owner of the Ploughbottom painting. Hudson was right. The painting had up until a few (4.) weeks/ minutes ago belonged to the family. However, after the last Lord Ploughbottom had died, impoverished and without any heirs, the executor of the estate had decided to sell all of the Ploughbottom's (5.) cars/property.
The (6.) estate/flat in the outskirts of London was up for sale as well as the entire inventory.
Mr Blighton had purchased the painting at the estate.
Elvira pulled into the (7.) lake/drive. She was (8.) astonished/bored.

The building, at least the outside, was flawless. This was not untypical for modern British nobility – keep the outside looking good, while inside the bankruptcy administrator was valuing the silver.
"I'm going to have a look at your old house, my lord," said Elvira to the painting of Lord Ploughbottom, that was leaning against the back seat. She had taken it with her, so that she could bring it back to the gallery on her way home. But that could wait.
Elvira went to the door and searched vainly for a doorbell. Instead she found an old-fashioned door knocker made of copper, in the form of two dice.

Übung 81: Übersetzen Sie ins Englische, um das Geheimwort zu enträtseln!

ÜBUNG 81 !

1. Kupfer _ _ _ _ ☐ _
2. makellos _ ☐ _ _ _ _ _ _
3. vergeblich ☐ _ _ _ _ _
4. Erbe _ _ ☐ _
5. bankrott _ _ _ _ ☐ _ _ _
6. Familiensitz _ _ _ ☐ _ _

Lösung: _ _ _ _ _ _

How fitting, thought Elvira as she knocked twice against the old wooden door.
Seconds later, a pale, old man with a large moustache opened the door.
He's trying to give his boring, bookkeeping face some distinction with that moustache, thought Elvira, but he failed.
The man had such a plain, ordinary face that one would forget five minutes later.
"What can I do for you?" the man asked.
"Hello. My name is Elvira Elliot. I called earlier."
"Of course, Miss Elliot. You wanted to view the remaining valuables that are for sale, right?"
Elvira nodded. She hadn't told the man that she was an insurance agent and was working on a case with Scotland Yard. Why make things unnecessarily complicated?
The man motioned her to come in.

"My name is Walter Nigma. I'm the executor of the Ploughbottom estate. There isn't much left, I'm afraid. The remaining valuable items have already been sold."

ÜBUNG 82

Übung 82: Übersetzen Sie ins Englische!

1. Ich werde die alten Gemälde überprüfen.

2. Er spazierte aus der Bank.

3. Miss Paddington hatte einen angenehmen Tag.

4. Der echte Arzt wurde an einen Stuhl gefesselt aufgefunden.

5. Wann wird er sich zur Ruhe setzen?

6. Dies war typisch für Versicherungsagenten.

"Oh, um, that's all right. I am only a historian looking for interesting sources," Elvira lied.

"I see," answered Nigma and glanced at Elvira with his expressionless face.

Übung 83: Welcher Satz ist die richtige Übersetzung?

1. Das Gemälde lehnte gegen die Wand.
   a) ☐ The painting is leaning against the wall.
   b) ☐ The painting leaned from the wall.
   c) ☐ The painting leaned against the wall.

2. Sie entdeckte eine alte Schatzkiste.
   a) ☐ She finded an old treasure chest.
   b) ☐ She found an old treasure chest.
   c) ☐ She finds an old treasure chest.

3. In 5 Minuten wird Hudson dieses Gesicht vergessen.
   a) ☐ Hudson will forget this face in 5 minutes.
   b) ☐ Since 5 minutes Hudson forgets his face.
   c) ☐ Hudson is forgetting this face in 5 minutes.

4. Ich habe Ihnen diese Woche schon geschrieben.
   a) ☐ I was writing you already during the week.
   b) ☐ I will write you already this week.
   c) ☐ I already wrote you this week.

5. Alles wird morgen verkauft.
   a) ☐ Everything will be sold tomorrow.
   b) ☐ Tomorrow everything will be selled.
   c) ☐ Everything is selling tomorrow.

"Please come in," he said and ushered her into the house. He held the door open for Elvira.
In the large hall, several tables had been set up, on which stood a few sculptures, yellowed books and porcelain dishes.

ÜBUNG 84 !

Übung 84: Setzen Sie ein sinnvolles Synonym ein!

"It does look rather (1. bare) ________," said Elvira, attempting to hide her disappointment. How among these pitiful remnants was she to find a (2. hint) ____________ about the painting?

Mr Nigma said nothing.

"How did the Ploughbottoms become so (3. without money) ______________?" asked Elvira, hoping that Nigma knew something about the family history that could give her a valuable clue.

The executor was not very talkative.

"Gambling," was all he said. "It ran in the family like an addiction. The Ploughbottoms were (4. always) ________________ trying to gamble away their (5. possessions) ______________."

Elvira sighed.

"It looks like they were successful."

"What do you mean?" asked Nigma.

Elvira shook her head. "Nothing. Do you mind if I look around?"

"Not at all."

One could hardly (6. notice) ____________ the shake of his head.

"Look around. I will be in the salon next door. I have to make some calculations about the sale value of the property."

"Have fun," said Elvira and smiled at the executor.
Elvira went to the tables and examined the family property. As an insurance agent, she knew a bit about antiques – these things only had sentimental value.
Elvira ran her finger over a small statue of Fortuna, the goddess of luck. Obviously, she had not aided the Ploughbottoms in their gambling addiction.
Next to the statue were a pile of old books. Elvira took the topmost and dusted off the cover: *Calculation of Probability for Gambling and Roulette, London 1867* was the title.
Obviously books promising a failsafe strategy for roulette went way back.
Elvira was just about to put the book back, when she noticed the smaller one that had laid under the one in her hand.

Übung 85: Setzen Sie die Sätze ins Passiv!

1. Hudson found the clue in the painting.

____

2. The Phantom steered the car.

____

3. The phoney bank director took the money.

____

4. Mr Nigma takes care of the Ploughbottom estate.

____

5. Elvira picked up the book.

____

It was bound in thick, dark leather printed with gold letters, whose glitter had faded.

Elvira gasped. “This looks very promising,” she whispered to herself.

On the book was printed *The Diary of Lord Ploughbottom*. Her fingers trembled with excitement as Elvira opened the book. If there wasn’t a clue to the painting here, then where else?

Übung 86: Wie heißt das Wort auf Deutsch?

1. executor ____________________
2. tremble ____________________
3. gambling ____________________
4. occasion ____________________
5. bad luck ____________________
6. addiction ____________________
7. cover ____________________
8. diary ____________________
9. handwriting ____________________
10. fade ____________________

The yellowing pages were filled with a small but elegant handwriting. Elvira sighed. It would take days to read the diary. If need be, she could surely buy the book for a few pounds from Mr Nigma, so that she could read it at home.
But it wouldn't hurt to take a little peek at it now.
Elvira skimmed over the pages. Lord Ploughbottom must have really been a passionate gambler. Most of his diary entries were devoted to various bets and games.
It's amazing that the Ploughbottoms didn't go bankrupt sooner, thought Elvira. The goddess of luck that was still standing nearby really didn't seem to have helped them much.
According to the diary entries, Lord Ploughbottom often lost at gambling and seldom won.
"Well, maybe he was lucky in love," murmured Elvira, shaking her head. She decided to expedite things by turning to the last page.

Übung 87: Welche Wörter stehen in Beziehung zueinander?

1. gambling	☐	source
2. sports car	☐	cover
3. family	☐	religion
4. painting	☐	entry
5. historian	☐	secretary
6. goddess	☐	money
7. diary	☐	heir
8. book	☐	Impressionism
9. furniture	☐	tyre

The entries ended abruptly on the 28th of March, 1697. The writing of the last entries was shaky, as if it cost the writer a great

effort to put the words on paper. Elvira deciphered the last sentence: *"I feel the consumption taking over my body, yet I will go peacefully from this world ..."*
The diary ended there.

ÜBUNG 88 !

Übung 88: Unterstreichen Sie die Antworten auf folgende Fragen im Text!

1. What did Lord Ploughbottom die of?
2. What indicated that the lord was excited in an earlier diary entry?
3. Why did Lord Ploughbottom think he would win that night?
4. What piece of paper would determine who owned the island?
5. What was the name of the island?

Poor man, thought Elvira. He, like many of his contemporaries, had fallen victim to tuberculosis. But that didn't solve the mystery. Elvira went back a few pages. The handwriting was different, not so shaky, as if the lord had written in great agitation.
Elvira bent over the yellow pages, glanced over the entries and gasped.
She felt her heart beating faster. It couldn't possibly be true.
Elvira reached into her purse and grabbed her mobile phone. She pounded in Hudson's office phone number.
"James," she cried, without waiting to say hello, "I think I know what was in the back of the painting. I have Lord Ploughbottom's diary here. Are you sitting down? I'll read it to you:

In spite of my increasing weakness, I will meet again with Lord Elword this evening to play at dice. For three weeks, Lord Elword

has beaten me. According to the rules of probability, luck must be on my side tonight. Since money is tight, I will bet part of the family estate – a remote piece of land of some value. I will issue a debt certificate to be given to the mayor of the island, upon which, the island will fall into possession of the certificate holder.
I hope my ancestors forgive me for betting old family property, but I am sure that I will be lucky tonight. Besides, the Isle of Man was always too draughty for me."

Übung 89: Ist das Wort richtig übersetzt?
Markieren Sie: richtig ✓ falsch –

1. consumption/Krebs
2. mobile phone/Handy
3. shorten/verlängern
4. abruptly/plötzlich
5. shaky/fest
6. riddle/Rätsel
7. skim/überfliegen
8. greet/verabschieden
9. probability/Wahrscheinlichkeit
10. debt/Schuld
11. dope/Panik

Elvira still couldn't believe it, even though she had already read the entry three times. Hudson was also silent on the other end.
"Did you hear that, James? Lord Ploughbottom bet the Isle of Man in a game of dice. The document hidden in the back of the portrait is the debt certificate. Whoever has this, just has to present it to the

Isle's mayor and the entire island is his! It's crazy, isn't it, James?" The mobile phone was silent. Either the inspector was speechless, or the connection had been terminated. Elvira looked at her display.

No reception appeared. Hopefully James had heard the most important part. She would drive immediately to Scotland Yard. She and Hudson had to stop the Phantom from reaching the Isle of Man with the debt certificate.

Then she realised that she couldn't just take the diary with her. She quickly went to the salon and quietly opened the door.

! ÜBUNG 90

Übung 90: Setzen Sie das richtige Verb in der korrekten Form ein!
(present, take over, support, grab, bet, devote, beat, forgive, lose)

1. He always __________ at dice.
2. Miss Paddington __________ Hudson yesterday at cards.
3. Can you __________ me for losing the estate?
4. He will __________ all his time to solving the case.
5. The Phantom wants to __________ the Isle of Man.
6. Last night, he __________ two horses in the dice game.
7. Elvira __________ Scotland Yard with art thefts.
8. The ghost __________ Hudson from behind.
9. If he __________ the certificate to the mayor, the property is his.

"Mr Nigma?" she called softly.

No one answered. The salon was empty. Elvira shrugged her shoulders and shut the door.

What can I do? she thought. She could always call the executor from the car and tell him that she had taken the diary.
Elvira raced through the main entrance, threw open the house door and dashed to her car.
The portrait of Lord Ploughbottom was still in the passenger's seat.

Übung 91: Wählen Sie die richtige Präposition!

ÜBUNG 91 !

1. _____ three weeks now, Lord Elword has beaten me.

   a) ☐ In b) ☐ For c) ☐ Of

2. Lord Ploughbottom is _____ debt.

   a) ☐ in b) ☐ on c) ☐ through

3. Hudson will bet _____ the black horse.

   a) ☐ to b) ☐ in c) ☐ on

4. Present the certificate _____ the mayor and its yours.

   a) ☐ to b) ☐ at c) ☐ against

5. Elvira looked _____ her rear view mirror.

   a) ☐ through b) ☐ upon c) ☐ in

6. "That was silly _____ you," she murmured.

   a) ☐ from b) ☐ of c) ☐ with

"That was really reckless of you, my dear lord, betting an entire island," she said as she moved to start the car. Suddenly, she noticed something moving in the rear view mirror. She whirled around in shock. In the back seat sat Mr Nigma with a smile on his face.

! ÜBUNG 92

Übung 92: Bilden Sie Wörter aus dem Buchstabenchaos!

His smile was treacherous, not at all fitting with the 1. vonseeac-tivr __________ (konservativ) bookeeper image.

"I'm sorry, if I've frightened you my 2. seadrte __________ (Beste)," said Nigma with a deep, sonorous voice. "But I'm afraid I just can't part with that diary so easily."

With lightning 3. espde __________ (Geschwindigkeit), the man pulled the 4. soutmchea __________ (Schnurrbart) off his face. A few pieces of 5. ugle __________ (Klebstoff) stuck on the fake moustache.

"I'm sorry, but I had to get rid of that troublesome thing. It 6. htci-se __________ (juckt). I hate to use disguises with facial hair."

"D-disguises," stuttered Elvira as she stared into the stranger's eyes. They were no longer pale blue, but deep brown.

He had obviously worn contact lenses before. "You mean, you're not Mr Nigma. You're …"
The man smiled.
"Absolutely right. The Phantom. We had the pleasure of meeting

already, when I was Mr Bixby. What won't one do in order to possess one little island. I assure you that what I must now do also brings me no pleasure."

Elvira's eyes widened.

"What are you going to do?" she cried and tried to open her door.

But the Phantom was faster and pressed a foul smelling handkerchief against her nose and mouth.

Chloroform rushed into her head.

She tried to tear his hand away from her face, but it was too late.

Darkness closed in around Elvira.

Inspector Hudson pressed the receiver against his ear.

"Elvira," he called, "are you still there?"

But the connection was still. The connection had been bad the whole time.

But Elvira's discovery was unbelievable. The Isle of Man!

No wonder the Phantom was so obsessed with getting a hold of the debt certificate.

The inspector thought it over.

Übung 93: Bilden Sie sinnvolle Sätze!

1. really Phantom Mr Nigma the be out turned to

___

2. was be found to salon the one in No

___

3. unbelievable The discovery be appeared to

___

ÜBUNG 93 !

4. barely could her understand Hudson

5. dead mobile The went phone all sudden a of

6. unconscious made drugs Elvira The

The Isle of Man lies in the Irish Sea, exactly between England and Ireland. Unlike England, this tiny island was never conquered by the Romans or the Normans and first became part of the British Empire in the 14th century.
The inspector opened his Internet connection and pulled up the CIA World-Factbook site, a public source from his colleagues in the American secret service.
Seconds later, a drawing of the island appeared on his screen. The island was 33 miles long, 13 miles wide and had a population of 74,000. He remembered it as being a very beautiful island.

ÜBUNG 94 !

Übung 94: Setzen Sie die Steigerungsform des Adjektivs ein!

1. He can draw ______________ (expressive) than she can.
2. Elvira is ______________ (young) than Miss Paddington.
3. The man with the scar was __________ (evil) than the other.
4. Sir Reginald feels __________ (bad) than Hudson.
5. That was the __________ (good) cup of tea I've ever had.
6. Lord Elword is __________ (rich) than Lord Ploughbottom.

7. It was the ___________ (bad) day of Hudson's life.

8. Miss Paddington is ___________ (funny) than Hudson.

9. Elvira is ___________ (tired) than Mr Blighton.

10. Madrid is ___________ (sunny) than London.

Now Hudson really had to sit down. If the debt certificate was valid, then the island was certainly worth millions of millions of pounds, if one could place a value on the island at all. The Phantom could not be allowed to reach the island.
The inspector tried to reach Elvira again. Then he dialled an internal number.
"Is this the dispatch office? I need a car to take me to Liverpool. And book me on a ferry to the Isle of Man."

Elvira awoke with a furry tongue. She needed a few moments to realise that her arms were tied behind her back. Her feet were also tied together with a thick rope.
The young lady let loose a very unladylike curse and looked around. She was in a large wooden building, where the floor was covered with straw. Probably a stable somewhere behind the estate.

Übung 95: Welches Wort ist das „schwarze Schaf"?

1. eyes, nose, jacket, foot ___________

2. car, ferry, rowing boat, yacht ___________

3. wood, iron, rubber, steel ___________

4. television, telephone, letter, e-mail ____________

5. paper, pen, kettle, pencil ____________

Elvira briefly considered calling for help, but decided not to. Apart from herself and the phoney executor, there seemed to be no-one on the estate. Besides, a cry for help would alert the Phantom – if he was still there.
Most likely, the master of disguise was already on his way to make good on the debt certificate and to take possession of the island.

ÜBUNG 96 !

Übung 96: Setzen Sie das richtige englische Verb ein!

Elvira needed something with which she could (1. schneiden) ____________ her bonds. She looked around.

The stable was cleared out. Everything pointed or sharp had already been (2. entfernen) ____________.

With some effort, she could (3. spüren) ____________ the pockets of her suit. She groaned. As far as she knew, all she had in them was a bag of peppermint candies and a lighter.

She (4. fallen) ____________ back in the straw with a disappointed sigh. Then (5. kommen) ____________ a burning idea, literally: She could (6. brennen) ____________ through the bonds!

Elvira struggled to sit up and (7. verdrehen) __________ her arms, in order to reach the lighter. She had the feeling that an enormous amount of time had (8. vorbeigehen) __________ before she was finally able to get the lighter out.

But at last she had it in her hand. She crawled away from the pile of straw, as she didn't want to set the whole stable on fire.

When she was far enough away, she placed the lighter in the right place behind her back. She searched for the flint and lit. She felt the heat from the small flame.

Now she had to be careful that the flame hit the rope and not her own hand. A few seconds later, a small cloud of smoke rose from behind her. Elvira put out the flame and waited a few seconds. She wanted to carefully melt the rope, as long as her hand was still in it. She repeated the process.

A few minutes later it happened. With a snap the last threads of the rope broke.

Elvira's hands were free. She quietly rejoiced and rubbed her aching wrists. After a few minutes, she had also undone the ropes around her ankles.

Elvira got up and carefully opened the stable door. It was slowly getting dark outside. Cautiously, she crept towards her sports car, still standing in front of the house.

The painting of the lord and his diary were still on the back seat. Elvira jumped in the car and sped away.

If she knew Hudson correctly, he was already on the way to the Isle of Man to stop the Phantom.

And she would help him. That was for sure.

Übung 97: Wie lautet das Wort auf Englisch?

1. pelzig ____________________
2. Geschmack ____________________
3. Handgelenk ____________________
4. Pferdestall ____________________
5. Gegenstand ____________________
6. Bonbon ____________________
7. Seil ____________________
8. Faust ____________________
9. Feuerzeug ____________________
10. Prozedur ____________________

The inspector stood on the deck of the ferry gazing at the silhouette of Liverpool. A few hours ago, he left London in a flurry in order to get a seat on the 'Pride of the Sea', that was to take him to the Isle of Man. In the meantime, he had repeatedly tried to contact Elvira on her mobile phone, but to no avail.

Übung 98: Was wird beschrieben?

1. The room where you can dance.

____

2. A piece of furniture that you sit on in the bar.

____

3. The room where meetings take place.

---

4. A large piece of furniture that several people can sit on.

---

5. The room where people sit together to talk or watch television.

---

6. A house where pictures are sold.

---

7. A place where you train your muscles.

---

8. An appliance used for cooking and baking.

---

9. An appliance with a tap used to wash your hands or dishes.

---

10. A piece of furniture with a door where you can keep your clothes.

The wail of the ship's sirens signalled that the ship was ready to depart. The inspector patted the inside pocket of his jacket.
The fact was, that Sir Reginald has insisted on Hudson carrying a firearm. One had to assume that the Phantom was also on his way to the island's capital, Douglas.

According to what Elvira had read out of the diary, the Phantom had to present the debt certificate to the mayor of the capital in person.
Hudson had taken precautions that would throw cold water on the master criminal's plans.

ÜBUNG 99

Übung 99: Gibt der Satz den richtigen Sachverhalt wieder? Markieren Sie: richtig ✓ falsch –

1. The meeting at the estate was the first time Elvira and the Phantom had seen each other.
2. The Phantom's real eye colour is brown.
3. The Phantom used carbon monoxide to make Elvira unconscious.
4. The capital of the Isle of Man is Dublin.
5. The inspector used the Internet to research.
6. The island is worth a great deal of money.
7. Hudson plans to take the ferry from Brighton.
8. Elvira burned through the ropes to free herself.
9. The Phantom had taken her car, the diary and the painting when he left the estate.

The inspector smiled grimly as he watched several sailors loose the ropes. Too bad Elvira couldn't be here, he thought.
At that moment, a familiar figure dashed onto the dock.
Inspector Hudson couldn't believe his eyes. It was Elvira Elliot running onto the ferry, with blowing hair and wild gestures.
Hudson moved quickly towards her. She was holding onto the railing and panting.
"My goodness, Elvira, did you run all the way here from London?"

"It feels like it, James. You have no idea what has happened to me since I last called. The Phantom kidnapped me, but I was able to get away."

Übung 100: Finden Sie das Lösungswort!

1. Hauptstadt _ _ □ _ _ _ _
2. sich beeilen □ _ _ _ _
3. Matrose _ □ _ _ _ _
4. entführen _ _ _ □ _ _
5. hecheln _ _ _ □
6. Anlegesteg _ □ _ _
7. Schusswaffe _ _ _ _ _ _ □

Lösung: _ _ _ _ _ _ _

Hudson looked at Elvira with concern.
"Oh my, Elvira. Are you all right? Did you get hurt?"
Elvira shook her head.
"Don't worry, James. It takes more than a faceless phantom to get rid of Elvira Elliot. But I'll tell you everything later. I want to go to my cabin and take a shower. Luckily I was able to use my mobile to book a cabin on the way here."
Hudson nodded.
"Of course, Elvira. Freshen up and get some rest. You can tell me

the whole story over dinner. We won't reach the Isle of Man until tomorrow morning anyway."
"Dinner sounds great, James."
With these words, Elvira disappeared into the ferry's interior. The inspector watched her go with admiration. What a woman!

! ÜBUNG 101

Übung 101: Unterstreichen Sie das richtige Wort!

Two hours later, Elvira and Hudson were already sitting over their dessert. Elvira had bought a new (1.) sloppy/elegant dress on board. An observer looking at her and the inspector could (2.) think/know that they were two tourists on a (3.) business/holiday cruise.
But the topic of (4.) dialogue/conversation was anything but trivial. Elvira recounted her run-in with the Phantom alias Mr Nigma.
"My (5.) compliments/scorn, Elvira," said Hudson, taking a sip of espresso. "You really tricked the Phantom. But we have to be on our guard. The Phantom will also be on his (6.) way/road to Douglas to give the mayor the debt certificate. He could be anywhere, disguised as anyone."
Both of them started as a man (7.) left/approached their table. It was just the steward bringing them their bill with a (8.) rude/polite nod. Could he be the Phantom?
Everything was possible, but here, in the (9.) full/empty dining room, nothing could happen to them.
Hudson reached for his (10.) handbag/wallet and handed the waiter a few banknotes.

"You don't mind if I pay, Elvira?" he asked.
"That's kind of you. I hope you can put it on your expense account."

"I'm afraid my expense account at Scotland Yard wouldn't even cover an espresso, not to mention this delicious meal. My compliments to the cook," said Hudson and glanced friendly at the waiter.

Elvira and Hudson stood up.

"Will you join me for a stroll on the deck, Elvira?" Hudson asked expectantly.

"A bit of exercise after dinner would do me good."

Elvira smiled and took his arm. "With pleasure, James."

Übung 102: Welche Worte haben dieselbe Bedeutung?

1.	tasty	☐ indicate
2.	trick	☐ eternal
3.	concerned	☐ relax
4.	tell	☐ delicious
5.	rest	☐ delay
6.	admiration	☐ outline
7.	signal	☐ cheat
8.	gun	☐ distant
9.	precaution	☐ worried
10.	believe	☐ respect
11.	silhouette	☐ recount
12.	leave	☐ preventative measures
13.	endless	☐ firearm
14.	far	☐ depart
15.	wait	☐ trust

"Do you think we will get there before the Phantom does, James?" asked Elvira worriedly. Hudson sighed.

"I hope so, Elvira. In any case, I have taken precautions so that the Phantom can't redeem the debt certificate. I shudder to think about what would happen if the entire Isle of Man were in the possession of a criminal."
Elvira looked at the inspector questioningly.
"What is the bastard thinking? I mean, as soon as he exposes himself by trying to redeem the certificate, you or the local authorities could arrest him!"
The inspector sighed.
"On what grounds? Scotland Yard and Interpol suspect that the Phantom is behind dozens of crimes, but we can't prove anything. We have no concrete evidence that the Phantom stole the portrait of Lord Ploughbottom. Or that he attacked you on the Ploughbottom estate. Anyone could have disguised themselves as the executor. That's what the Phantom would argue. All he needs to do is stroll into the town hall in any disguise he chooses and present the certificate. It's not a crime to run around in a disguise."

ÜBUNG 103 !

Übung 103: Übersetzen Sie den Satz ins Englische!

1. Elvira wollte ihm das Tagebuch persönlich vorlesen.

____

2. Die Matrosen stehen auf dem Anlegesteg.

____

3. Wirst du den ganzen Weg nach Hause zu Fuß gehen?

____

4. Hudson benutzte sein Handy, um eine Fahrkarte zu buchen.

____

5. Der Gefangene wird in den Gerichtssaal geleitet.

____

6. Der Kellner wird die Nachspeise auftragen.

____

Elvira looked gravely at James.
“I never thought of it that way. But you’re right. Even if we can prove that the Phantom stole the portrait, he will spend maybe a year in jail, and then come out as one of the world’s richest men. Theoretically, he could declare the island as his private property and create his own country.”
“I’d rather not think about it. Let’s enjoy this lovely evening at sea.”

Übung 104: Welche Antwort passt zur Frage?

1. What are you reading?
   a) ☐ A song by the Beatles.
   b) ☐ A ballet with Baryshnikov.
   c) ☐ A poem by John Donne.

2. What would you like to have for lunch?
   a) ☐ I will have a traditional English breakfast.
   b) ☐ Ice cream.
   c) ☐ I would like a tuna salad sandwich.

3. Why are you on the ferry to the Isle of Man?
   a) ☐ I want to see Buckingham Palace.
   b) ☐ I have business there.
   c) ☐ I want to go to Cornwall.

4. Where are you going on holiday?
   a) ☐ We are going to Thailand.
   b) ☐ We are going to the bank.
   c) ☐ We are going to work in Bangkok.

5. What is your favourite film?
   a) ☐ *The Magic Flute.*
   b) ☐ *Four Weddings and a Funeral.*
   c) ☐ The *Mona Lisa.*

Hudson and Elvira took in the fresh night air.
The stars shone over the Irish Sea, and the British flag waved in the breeze on the ship's bow.
"What a beautiful night," said Hudson softly. "On such a night, one could be tempted to forget crime."
Before Elvira could answer, a shadow appeared out of the darkness.

ÜBUNG 105 !

Übung 105: Setzen Sie das richtige Pronomen ein!

"But crime doesn't forget 1. ____________!" the shadow shouted.

Hudson and Elvira took a step backwards, shocked.

In front of 2. ____________ was a broad-shouldered sailor with a small club in 3. __________ paws.

The inspector instinctively reached for the pistol in his pocket, but the stranger was quicker. Before 4. __________ could pull his gun, the club was crashing down.

The inspector managed to avoid the treacherous blow with a clever step aside.

The sailor only grunted and got ready to strike again.

Elvira looked around 5. _____________.

At this late hour, 6. __________________ were alone on deck.

Elvira knew, that if 7. _____________ tried to call for help, the drone of the ship's engines would drown out 8. ________ voice.

The sailor aimed his club at the inspector again. Hudson groaned in pain as the club hit his arm, but it was still better then getting a blow on the head.

Hudson shrank backwards and thereby let down his guard for a fraction of a second.

The attacker didn't need any more. He rushed forward and grabbed the inspector's throat.

The man was amazingly strong, but he hadn't counted on Elvira Elliot.

She took her handbag and sent it crashing down on the sailor's head several times.

More surprised than hurt, the sailor whipped his head around and stared at Elvira in astonishment.

ÜBUNG 106 !

Übung 106: Bilden Sie sinnvolle Wörter aus dem Buchstabenchaos!

1. SPWA (Pranken) ______________________
2. CRAGE (Anmut) ______________________
3. ACBKRWASD (rückwärts) ______________________
4. CELEADR (erklären) ______________________
5. PTMTDEE (versucht) ______________________
6. SGGLETRU (Kampf) ______________________
7. BLUC (Knüppel) ______________________
8. ASRNRGTE (Fremde) ______________________
9. DREEME (einlösen) ______________________
10. TRARES (verhaften) ______________________

Hudson took advantage of this distraction to give the sailor a punch in the stomach, but the guy was really muscular.
At least the punch made the sailor let go of Hudson's throat.
"What the …," moaned the sailor, as he tried to stand upright.
A fraction of a second later, Elvira's handbag slammed against the sailor's nose.
The sailor groaned again, looked at Hudson and Elvira undecidedly, and then stormed away.
Elvira wanted to run after him, but Hudson restrained her.
"Wait. By the time we catch up with him inside the ship, he will have already slipped into a new disguise."

Übung 107: Setzen Sie jeweils das erste Wort in den Genitiv!

ÜBUNG 107 !

1. Elvira/handbag ________________
2. men/suits ________________
3. inspectors/offices ________________
4. James/health ________________
5. children/stories ________________
6. thieves/crimes ________________
7. cell/bars ________________

Elvira sighed.
The inspector brought Elvira to her cabin and waited, until he heard her lock the door from the inside. Then he went to his own cabin and prepared himself for bed.
But even with the peaceful rocking of the waves, it took a long time before Hudson fell asleep.
Something about the attack by the sailor was fishy.

Übung 108: Beantworten Sie die Fragen zum Text!

ÜBUNG 108 !

1. What was the name of the ferry Hudson took from Liverpool?

____

2. Was he able to reach Elvira on her mobile again?

____

3. What did the inspector wish for that immediately came true?

4. What did Elvira want to do as soon as she was on the ship?

Inspector Hudson awoke before his little travel alarm clock could ring. The weather had obviously got worse, and the ferry rocked between the waves.

Luckily, Hudson was not prone to seasickness.

Before he left his cabin to get Elvira for breakfast, he took another look at the display on his mobile. Ever since he departed, he had tried to call Sir Reginald to report, but clearly there was no reception here on the high sea.

Hudson sighed, but wasn't too upset. As far as he knew, the Isle of Man had been selected as a test region for the new UMTS mobile network a few months ago. There shouldn't be a problem connecting with the mainland.

Still on his guard, Hudson left his cabin and reached Elvira's in a few steps.

Hudson smiled to himself as he knocked on Elvira's door.

! ÜBUNG 109

Übung 109: Wie heißt die Redewendung auf Deutsch?

1. It can wait.	☐ Liebhaberwert
2. once in a while	☐ im wahrsten Sinne des Wortes
3. go to great lengths	☐ die Suppe versalzen
4. sentimental value	☐ ab und zu
5. go way back	☐ gewaltige Anstrengungen unternehmen

6. literally	☐	in der Familie liegen
7. throw cold water on	☐	Es hat Zeit.
8. run in the family	☐	eine lange Geschichte haben
9. knock on wood	☐	wie ein Vogel im Käfig
10. like a bird in the cage	☐	auf Holz klopfen

Elvira opened the door with a smile. She also did not seem to be affected by the rough sea.

"Good morning, Elvira. Did you sleep well? All ready for the big day?"

"And how!" answered Elvira. "The hunt for the Phantom can start right now. The ugly ghost should be prepared for a little trouble."

Hudson held the door open for Elvira.

She locked her cabin door behind her and followed the inspector into the dining room. The stormy sea had kept most of the other passengers from breakfast. Hudson and Elvira chose one of the many free spots near the window.

While they drank their tea, they watched the waves spew their foam against the windows.

Übung 110: Ersetzen Sie die unterstrichenen Begriffe durch ein passenderes Wort!

Elvira glanced at the inspector over the edge of her teacup.

"Do you think we will catch the Phantom before it is too early 1. ________________?"

"I want 2. ________________ so, Elvira. In any way 3. __________,

I've taken precautions, so that the Phantom, in whatever disguise he may appear, doesn't make it to the lawyer 4. ________________. I've alerted the local police, to guard the mayor, Mr Manxon, around the clock. And the bonus 5. ______________ certificate is only valid if presented in person."

Elvira smiled dissatisfied 6. ________________.

"That should be too much 7. ______________ to stop the Phantom. And we still have enough time to look for and apprehend the villain."

"I hope so, my dear. But I have a good 8. ________________ feeling, that the Phantom still has a trump to play."

An hour later, the 'Pride of the Sea' laid anchor at the Isle of Man. Dark clouds were appearing on the horizon. Hudson didn't believe in omens, but the weather seemed to sense that something evil was afoot.
Hudson and Elvira were greeted by a young police officer.
"You are certainly Inspector Hudson and Miss Elliot," said the young man. "It's my job to bring you to city hall immediately."
Inspector Hudson shook the policeman's hand and looked at him sceptically.
"Very kind of you, but can I see your badge? Not to be rude ..."

Übung 111: Wie heißt der englische idiomatische Ausdruck?

1. improvisieren	☐ cost an arm and a leg
2. todsicher	☐ put oneself out
3. Glück haben	☐ sold up the river
4. zufällig	☐ play it by ear
5. chaotisch	☐ get lucky
6. extrem teuer sein	☐ at sixes and sevens
7. Umstände machen	☐ by chance
8. betrogen	☐ not my cup of tea
9. nicht mein Fall	☐ failsafe

"No problem, sir. My department already warned me that you would be suspicious. However, I have no idea what this is all about."

Hudson nodded. It was probable that the police in the lower ranks only received the information that was absolutely necessary, in order to avoid panic. After all, the island was about to be taken possession of by an unscrupulous criminal.

The inspector nodded at the police officer and gave him back his badge.

Übung 112: Welche Wörter haben die gegenteilige Bedeutung?

1. villain	☐ firm
2. unscrupulous	☐ slow
3. asleep	☐ uneven
4. rapid	☐ hero
5. muscular	☐ carefree
6. undecided	☐ awake

7.	restrain	☐	stormy
8.	smooth	☐	flabby
9.	tranquil	☐	moral
10.	worried	☐	release

"Everything is OK, officer. Please bring us to city hall as quickly as possible."

"Everything is working out splendidly," Elvira remarked and looked out of the window. The first rain drops dashed against the glass.

"Wait and see," murmured the inspector, "... wait and see."

ÜBUNG 113 !

Übung 113: Setzen Sie die Sätze ins Aktiv!

1. Elvira was attacked by Mr Nigma sincerely.

____

2. The debt certificate was possessed by the Phantom.

____

3. The gun was carried by Hudson.

____

4. Elvira was drugged by an unknown man.

____

5. Elvira's car is driven by Miss Paddington.

____

6. The beer will be drunk by Matches Marconi in the dive.

---

7. By whom will the letter be written?

A few minutes later, the police car stopped in front of the Douglas city hall. Hudson and Elvira got out. In spite of the increasing rain, they took a few moments to admire the Victorian building.
"Quite a beautiful building," observed the inspector. "What a pity that it should fall into the Phantom's hands."

Übung 114: Welche ist die richtige Übersetzung?

ÜBUNG 114 !

1. Hudson blickt über die Reling.
   a) ☐ Hudson leaned over the railing.
   b) ☐ Hudson looked over the railing.
   c) ☐ Hudson looked at the railing.

2. Es wird ein stürmischer Tag auf dem Meer sein.
   a) ☐ It will be a stormy day at sea.
   b) ☐ It was a stormy day in the sea.
   c) ☐ It will be a stormy day on top of the sea.

3. Die meisten Passagiere vermeiden das Frühstück.
   a) ☐ Most passengers allowed breakfast.
   b) ☐ Most passengers avoided breakfast.
   c) ☐ Most passengers avoid breakfast.

4. Sicherheitsvorkehrungen werden getroffen.
   a) ☐ Secure measures are taken.
   b) ☐ Security precautions will be taken.
   c) ☐ Security turns will be taken.

5. Er soll den Bürgermeister nie erreichen.
   a) ☐ He will never reach the mayor.
   b) ☐ He should never reach the mayor.
   c) ☐ He could never reach the mayor.

"But we're here to stop that, aren't we, James?" replied Elvira. Hudson nodded. They followed the young policeman, who led them through the imposing building to the mayor's office.
Two security guards were posted in front of the door. They nodded at Inspector Hudson and Elvira and opened the large wooden door. A large, jovial looking man stood up from his desk and approached them.

ÜBUNG 115 !

Übung 115: Bilden Sie Wörter aus dem Buchstabenchaos!

He was clearly of Irish ancestry. On his head, raged red-blond 1. surcl ____________ (Locken), that could not be tamed by a 2. obcm ____________ (Kamm).

"Miss Elliot and Mr Hudson from Scotland Yard," he cried with visible 3. fereli ____________ (Erleichterung), "I'm 4. yphap ____________ (glücklich) that you're here to catch this Phantom. Your boss told me the 5. ienret ____________ (ganze) story. Ever since then, I've been afraid to leave my office."

The insurance agent reached into her handbag and pulled something out.
"Don't worry. The game is up. You can go where you like. The fact is, that I will even have to ask that you leave *my* office immediately!"
The inspector's eyes widened. Before he could say or do anything, Elvira had pressed a yellowed piece of paper into the hands of the speechless mayor.
Lord Ploughbottom's debt certificate!
"Elvira, what …?" stammered Hudson. But Elvira simply smiled coldly at him.

Übung 116: Unterstreichen Sie das richtige Verb! Achten Sie dabei auf die Situationshinweise!

ÜBUNG 116 !

1. Can/May you speak English? (Fähigkeit)
2. May/Shall I accompany you on the case? (Bitte um Erlaubnis)
3. Shall/Can we go to the cinema? (Vorschlag)
4. You should/may call your mother more often. (Verpflichtung)
5. He may/can come tonight. (Wahrscheinlichkeit)
6. He shall/should leave for Douglas tomorrow. (Zukunft)
7. They should/can arrive around 7 o'clock. (Schätzung)
8. They may/can not smoke here. (Verbot)
9. Can/May you pass the butter? (Bitte)
10. Should/Shall we go? (Frage nach einer Meinung)

"Thank you, inspector, for leading me directly to Mr Manxon. Without your help, I would have had a much harder time reaching him," said Elvira, with a voice that didn't sound like her.

Hudson involuntarily took a step back.

"You're … the Phantom!"

"Of course," answered Elvira. "Who else?"

The inspector became dizzy.

It all seemed to add up! He should have realised it earlier. The phoney 'Elvira' had said that she had booked a cabin using her mobile phone, while the inspector had tried to call her at least half-a-dozen times on her mobile. Also, the sailor last night had reacted to Elvira's attack with shock, probably because the Phantom himself had ordered the attack on Hudson.

ÜBUNG 117 !

Übung 117: Ist das Idiom richtig übersetzt worden? Markieren Sie: richtig ✓ falsch –

1. believe one's eyes/seinen Augen nicht trauen
2. to be on one's guard/locker sein
3. fishy/verdächtig
4. still have a trump to play/nichts mehr machen können
5. have a hard time/es schwer haben
6. to beat around the bush/Tacheles reden
7. to be on the go/auf Achse
8. to jump the gun/bedacht handeln
9. Hold your horses!/Bleib cool!
10. out-fox/täuschen

Hudson was *supposed* to believe that the Phantom was disguised as the sailor – in order to divert suspicion from the phoney Elvira!

The Phantom pulled a lifelike latex mask from his face and threw it on the floor.
The man behind the mask was about 35 years old, with short, dark hair. He was good looking, except for the long scar that ran across his face.
"Y-you'll never get away with that," stuttered Hudson as he instinctively reached for his weapon.
The Phantom only stared at him with pity.
"Forget your weapon. You are on my land, and you have no proof against me. And now, get out of my office before I have you thrown out!"
The inspector shrank back.

Übung 118: Beantworten Sie die Fragen zum Text!

ÜBUNG 118 !

1. What did Hudson notice about his mobile phone while at sea?

____

2. Why did many of the passengers not come to breakfast?

____

3. Why was the inspector not sure that his security precautions were enough?

____

4. What were these precautions?

____

5. Who did the Phantom disguise himself as?

____

Elvira Elliot – the real Elvira Elliot – sat in her sports car and dialled the inspector's number for the hundredth time.

Ever since she barely missed the ferry, she had been trying desperately to contact Hudson.

Elvira stared at the painting of the smiling Lord Ploughbottom on her back seat.

Finally, a dial tone.

A few hundred miles away, Hudson's phone started ringing in his jacket pocket.

The Phantom raised an eyebrow.

"Don't hesitate to answer it, inspector," he said. "I don't want to be rude. Finish your call and leave my office, and my island!"

Then he smiled. "I hope it isn't your boss asking for an update."

ÜBUNG 119 !

Übung 119: Übersetzen Sie die Sätze ins Englische!

1. Das Gespräch war alles andere als lustig.

____

2. Im Moment nähert er sich langsam dem Tisch.

____

3. Wo kann ich diesen Coupon einlösen?

____

4. Jemand trat aus dem Schatten hervor.

____

5. Hudson wird die Ablenkung zum eigenen Vorteil nutzen.

____

6. Wir werden ihn nie einholen!

7. Er ist französischer Abstammung.

Hudson pressed the phone to his ear. It wasn't Sir Reginald. It was Elvira, the real Elvira.
"James! At last! You'll never believe what happened to me!"
"Elvira …"
"Listen to me, James. I solved the case. Do you remember the portrait of Lord Ploughbottom? It shows him smiling with a pair of dice in his hand. Both dice are showing a six! He hit the jackpot, so to say!"
"Elvira, what?"

Übung 120: Bilden Sie sinnvolle Sätze!

1. rocked waves the ferry The

2. clouds the gathered sky in Storm

3. Elvira The Elliot the presented letter phoney

4. with Are familiar the you Picasso of works?

5. full Sir a Reginald wants report

____

6. scar The was good-looking had Phantom but a

____

"No wait! That gave me an idea. I read Lord Ploughbottom's diary again. James, the Ploughbottoms were gambling addicted losers. That's why we never had the idea that they could ever get lucky! Of course, Lord Ploughbottom bet the Isle of Man. But this time, James, this time he won!"

The inspector couldn't believe his ears.

"Won," he repeated. "You mean …"

"Lord Ploughbottom diced with his friend Lord Elword for the island – and won the game. On this evening, by the way of exception, it wasn't Ploughbottom who lost a fortune, but Elword. The debt certificate is totally worthless!"

The inspector glanced at the Phantom, who stood frozen behind the mayor's desk.

The word 'won' had not escaped him.

ÜBUNG 121 !

Übung 121: Wie heißt das Wort auf Deutsch?

1.	fortune	☐	falsch
2.	prevent	☐	Freizeichen
3.	ancestry	☐	verhindern
4.	baffled	☐	Volltreffer
5.	involuntarily	☐	würfeln

6.	phony	☐	Bescheinigung
7.	instigate	☐	Ausnahme
8.	life-like	☐	süchtig
9.	pity	☐	Tagebuch
10.	territory	☐	Mitleid
11.	barely	☐	Vermögen
12.	desperately	☐	Bericht
13.	dial tone	☐	kaum
14.	report	☐	Abstammung
15.	jackpot	☐	verzweifelt
16.	diary	☐	unwillkürlich
17.	addicted	☐	anstiften
18.	dice	☐	Boden
19.	certificate	☐	lebensecht
20.	exception	☐	verdutzt

"Thank you, Elvira. I'll call you back," said the inspector. And before Elvira had a chance to protest, Hudson hung up.

The confidence had vanished from the criminal's face. He went pale.

"I think you know what that telephone call was about, old boy. I arrest you for attempted fraud!"

The Phantom shrank back.

"That is ridiculous! You … you have no proof."

Hudson smiled.

"Well, you did try to take possession of an island using a worthless piece of paper. I'm sure, when we have a quiet moment to take your fingerprints, that other crimes can be proved against you."

Übung 122: Welches Wort ist das „schwarze Schaf"?

1. nail, sunshine, thunder, storm ____________________

2. guard, security, lock, access ____________________

3. tree, wood, rose, oak ____________________

4. thriller, sonata, soap opera, quiz show ____________________

5. parody, satire, fantasy, power ____________________

6. dismiss, sack, promote, give notice ____________________

7. detached house, semi-detached house, terraced house, staircase ____________________

Hudson approached the Phantom with quick steps. Mr Manxon also rushed toward him. As the two men cornered him, the Phantom took a step back against the wall. He pressed against an ornate stained glass window with the crest of the Isle on it.

Übung 123: Setzen Sie das richtige Verb in der korrekten Form ein!

Hudson (1. ziehen) ____________ his weapon and took another step towards the Phantom.

"It's not over yet, Hudson," he (2. fauchen) ____________.

“We will see each other again. From now on, you’ll never be able to (3. vertrauen) ____________ anyone!”

With this threat, the Phantom (4. drehen) ____________ his back to the inspector and (5. springen) ____________ out the window. Coloured shards of glass (6. fliegen) ____________ through the room.

Hudson and the mayor protected their eyes and raced to the broken window.
The Phantom had vanished.
“Damn!” said the inspector.
“Don’t make such a big deal about it, inspector. You saved the Isle of Man and its inhabitants from the clutches of a criminal. That is the most important thing!”
Hudson nodded.
“You’re right, mayor. For now, we can be happy with the results. But one thing makes me nervous.”
“Do you mean the Phantom’s threats?” asked the mayor worriedly.
Hudson smiled.
“No, I can live with that. The bigger problem is that I have to confess to Elvira Elliot that I actually was able to confuse the Phantom and her …”

THE END

Abschlusstest

Übung 1: Nennen Sie ein Synonym für die folgenden Wörter!

1. criminal ____________________
2. picture ____________________
3. tunnel ____________________
4. phoney ____________________
5. shout ____________________
6. phantom ____________________
7. risky ____________________
8. safety ____________________
9. astonishing ____________________
10. nice ____________________

Übung 2: Setzen Sie das Verb in der korrekten Form ein!

1. Hudson could not (htcca) __________ the Phantom.
2. Yesterday, Miss Paddington (kema) __________ tea for Elvira.
3. Tomorrow, Sir Reginald (eavel) __________ for Leeds.
4. Hudson (lelt) __________ me two days ago.
5. (Mya) __________ I borrow your car?

6. Hudson (ntozie) __________ the thief five minutes ago.

7. Lord Ploughbottom (csrbbile) _________ in his diary every day.

8. Who has (skpea) __________ well about London?

9. In two weeks, I (tsrat) ________________ reading "The Hound of the Baskervilles".

10. Last year, we (vertal) __________ to the Provence on holiday.

Übung 3: Setzen Sie die Sätze vom Passiv ins Aktiv und umgekehrt!

1. Elvira eats the biscuit.

____

2. The Isle of Man was saved by Inspector Hudson.

____

3. The painting was copied by Jimmy Coltrane.

____

4. Who booked the ticket for the ferry?

____

5. Elvira filled her car with petrol.

____

6. The novel was read by Miss Paddington.

____

Übung 4: Wählen Sie den passenden Ausdruck für die jeweilige Situation!

1. You meet someone in the morning.
   a) ☐ Nice tomorrow.
   b) ☐ Good early day.
   c) ☐ Good morning.

2. Someone invites you to dinner and you can't go.
   a) ☐ I'm sorry but I have another engagement.
   b) ☐ Thanks, I would love to come.
   c) ☐ No, I don't want to come.

3. You like your friend's new dress.
   a) ☐ That's a hideous dress you have on.
   b) ☐ That's a lovely dress you have on.
   c) ☐ That's a strange dress you have on.

Übung 5: Ist der Satz richtig übersetzt?
Markieren Sie: richtig ✓ falsch –

1. Miss Paddington fährt jeden Tag mit dem Bus./Miss Paddington takes the bus every day.
2. Hudson arbeitet bei Scotland Yard seit 5 Jahren./Hudson works for Scotland Yard since 5 years.
3. Ich mache kein Geschäfte mit Gaunern./I don't make business with thieves.
4. Das Phantom könnte zurückkehren./The Phantom could return.
5. Elvira kann Französisch und Spanisch./Elvira can French and Spanish.

Übung 6: Ordnen Sie die Wörter den richtigen Überbegriffen zu!

a) to brake
b) chancellor
c) cancer
d) humanism
e) exhibition
f) deaf
g) harp
h) density
i) fuel
j) instalment
k) to purchase
l) exhausted
m) prehistoric
n) data processing
o) sculpture
p) surgeon

1. Wirtschaft ________________

2. Technik ________________

3. Kunst/Musik ________________

4. Geschichte/Politik ________________

5. Medizin ________________

Übung 7: Wie lautet die Übersetzung?

1. Steuern hinterziehen	☐	reorganize
2. eine Rechnung stellen	☐	compensation claim
3. Überstunden machen	☐	render an account
4. umorganisieren	☐	work overtime
5. Schadenersatz	☐	avoid tax
6. das neueste Modell	☐	trademark
7. Markenzeichen	☐	the latest model
8. eine Rechnung begleichen	☐	settle a bill

Lösungen

Übung 1: 1. day 2. week 3. half an hour 4. month 5. dozen 6. hour 7. year
Übung 2: 1. pile 2. sigh 3. fraud 4. mystery 5. evaluation 6. annoying 7. case 8. avoid 9. file
Übung 3: 1. worker 2. few 3. frown 4. one after the other 5. knowledge 6. healthy 7. lacking
Übung 4: 1. epidemic 2. immune system 3. routine case 4. wit 5. scene of the crime
Übung 5: 2. expert 3. colleagues 4. crime 5. housekeeper 6. receiver
Übung 6: 1. private detective 2. policeman (or police officer) 3. lawyer 4. accountant 5. author (or writer) 6. art dealer 7. judge 8. insurance agent 9. auctioneer
Übung 7: 1. a, f 2. b, g 3. c, d 4. e, h
Übung 8: 1. to 2. in 3. at 4. on 5. with 6. around 7. from
Übung 9: 1. falsch 2. richtig 3. falsch 4. richtig 5. falsch 6. falsch 7. richtig
Übung 10: was – to be, dressed – to dress, stared – to stare, fell – to fall, was – to be, executed – to execute, could – can, were – to be, held – to hold, showed – to show
Übung 11: 2. mugged 3. struck 4. raped 5. smuggled 6. sought out 7. took revenge 8. kidnapped 9. robbed 10. hijacked 11. swore 12. found a clue 13. dug 14. clung
Übung 12: 1. up-to-date 2. clue 3. inspect 4. damaged 5. unharmed 6. strange
Übung 13: 1. police force 2. keep under observation 3. bank robber 4. genetic fingerprint 5. protection money 6. diplomatic relations 7. secret agent 8. in civilian clothes 9. pistol shot 10. code name 11. sign a treaty 12. fire brigade 13. picture frame 14. oil paint 15. water colour 16. pastel crayon
Übung 14: 1. Because she was an expert on art. 2. Two dice, both showing the number six. 3. Picasso and Monet. 4. Because the painting was not worth as much money as the other two. 5. An anonymous artist. 6. How the thieves entered the building.
Übung 15: 1. c 2. b 3. b 4. c 5. c
Übung 16: 2. The sinks were torn from the walls by the thieves. 3. The hole was inspected by Hudson. 4. The tiles were moved by Elvira. 5. The damage is seen by Mr Blighton. 6. Notes are taken by the inspector.
Übung 17: 1. klettern 2. Loch 3. gefährlich 4. Schacht 5. Taschenlampe 6. folgen 7. feucht 8. klebrig 9. vertraut
Übung 18: 1. forensics 2. clues 3. conspiratorially 4. Then 5. ray 6. choice 7. forward
Übung 19: 1. asked/for help 2. trampled 3. smell 4. shine 5. hesitated 6. crawl
Übung 20: Adverbien: direkt/directly, genau/exactly, endlich/finally
Adjektive: alt/old, dunkel/dark, schmal/narrow, enorm/enormous, verwüstet/wasted, sprachlos/speechless

Übung 21: 1. Hudson's hunch was correct. 2. A rat is crawling across the floor. 3. He does not have a flashlight. 4. The tunnel is dangerous. 5. Who destroyed the bathroom? 6. Almost everyone at Scotland Yard has the flu.
Übung 22: 1. garage 2. reply 3. sculpture 4. safe 5. nervous 6. bar 7. spit
Übung 23: 1. May I compliment you? 2. You look lovely today. 3. How about something to eat? 4. Here's to you!
Übung 24: 1. excursion 2. accompany 3. remain 4. bother 5. surface 6. forensics 7. maternal 8. invitation 9. manners 10. impatient
Übung 25: 1. a sip of tea 2. a gang of thieves 3. sum of money 4. a piece of advice 5. a clump of dirt 6. a spot of paint 7. a glass of wine 8. a pound of butter 9. a gust of wind 10. a ray of light
Übung 26: 1. looked 2. fastened 3. seemed 4. make out 5. stared 6. fought
Übung 27: 1. richtig 2. falsch 3. falsch 4. richtig 5. falsch 6. falsch 7. falsch 8. richtig 9. richtig 10. falsch
Übung 28: 1. ghost 2. particular 3. network 4. middle 5. notice 6. replaced 7. entrance 8. perfect 9. building 10. snapped
Übung 29: 1. thieves 2. scenes 3. halves 4. mice 5. wolves 6. lights 7. tunnels 8. loaves
Übung 30: 1. Ich denke da an eine bestimmte Situation. 2. Sie hat es aus Freundschaft getan, nicht des Geldes wegen. 3. Er hat Elviras Bekanntschaft letztes Jahr in London gemacht. 4. Der Detektiv schüttelte den Kopf. 5. Mir wäre es lieber, wenn du zu Hause bliebest. 6. Pass auf dich auf. 7. Miss Paddington lächelte in sich hinein. 8. Der Inspector stottert oft.
Übung 31: 1. intruder 2. resolute 3. baseball bat 4. fear 5. familiar 6. unbearable 7. doorway
Übung 32: 1. prefer 2. fanatical 3. thoughtful 4. purse 5. ghost 6. reach 7. breath 8. bacon 9. intruder 10. frighten 11. recognize 12. smell
Lösung: Ploughbottom
Übung 33: 1. sense 2. afraid 3. circles 4. prison 5. unpleasant 6. looked 7. chest 8. dust
Übung 34: 1. return 2. important 3. incompetent 4. fresh 5. multiple 6. uninterested 7. worthless 8. independent 9. husband 10. breakfast
Übung 35: 1. fence 2. construction site 3. convince 4. search warrant 5. tools 6. skeleton
Übung 36: 1. The inspector climbed the lop-sided steps. 2. The moon bathed the steel girders in light. 3. Hudson did not convince the night watchman. 4. The intruder entered the property. 5. A security company patrolled the construction site. 6. The judge issued a search warrant. 7. Nobody used the machines. 8. The flashlight shone on the station.
Übung 37: 1. c 2. a 3. b 4. a 5. c

Übung 38: 1. socially 2. suspiciously 3. well 4. heartily 5. sinisterly 6. illegally 7. carefully 8. rustily 9. actually 10. regularly
Übung 39: 1. stretch 2. wheel around 3. glow 4. mislead 5. reflect 6. rush
Übung 40: 1. sleepy 2. tune 3. co-workers 4. lately 5. picture 6. asset 7. rich 8. competitor 9. curious
Übung 41: 1. People spend a lot of money on art. 2. Elvira had to wait a long time. 3. She called many art dealers. 4. Hudson doesn't like Picasso. 5. Hudson thought he saw a ghost. 6. A scream was heard. 7. Many collectors shop in London.
Übung 42: another time/again, found/discovered, yelled/shouted, lovely/beautiful, thankful/grateful, thruthful/honest, dreadful/terrible
Übung 43: 1. b 2. c 3. a 4. b 5. c
Übung 44: 1. ranch 2. bricks 3. autumn 4. insurance 5. sympathy 6. country 7. waitress
Übung 45: 1. falsch 2. falsch 3. richtig 4. falsch 5. richtig 6. richtig 7. falsch 8. richtig 9. falsch 10. richtig
Übung 46: 1. nodded 2. course 3. stolen 4. leave 5. expensive 6. miss 7. flight
Übung 47: 1. at 2. at 3. from 4. on 5. in 6. on 7. to 8. to 9. out 10. with
Übung 48: 1. nett, Art 2. Ball, Tanzabend 3. verlassen, Wüste 4. Rennen, Rasse 5. Miene, meines 6. lieben, gleich 7. Kompliment, loben
Übung 49: 1. There must be a logical explanation. 2. Miss Paddington believes in ghosts. 3. The rattle of the train was heard again. 4. Her eyes glowed in the dark. 5. Did anyone see the ghost? 6. Elvira was frightened by Hudson's disguise. 7. Hudson smiled as he saw Elvira coming. 8. Elvira asked questions and waited for the answers. 9. Why is Mr Bixby smiling? 10. He asked the waitress for a whiskey.
Übung 50: 1. That the ghosts of passengers haunted the tunnels. 2. Because he didn't have a search warrant. 3. Because he thought criminals would refuse to give him information if he came to them as a member of Scotland Yard. 4. A ghost. 5. Every time a train passed, the 'ghost' appeared.
Übung 51: 1. quiet/noisy 2. supernatural/normal 3. yell/whisper 4. float/sink 5. appear/vanish 6. logical/irrational 7. coincidental/planned 8. lift/drop 9. effective/useless 10. unwanted/welcome 11. hide/reveal 12. enjoy/dislike 13. worn/new
Übung 52: 1. as 2. to 3. In 4. after 5. to 6. during 7. away 8. from
Übung 53: 1. tube 2. pulse 3. rope 4. draught 5. scarecrow 6. pub 7. hidden 8. owner 9. midnight 10. license
Übung 54: 1. b 2. a 3. c 4. b 5. a 6. b 7. b
Übung 55: hinter/behind, schweigen/silenced, genannt/alias, ohrenbetäubend/deafening, Gespräche/conversation, fettig/greasy, Kumpel/mate, kahl/bald
Übung 56: 1. catch 2. banknote 3. pickpocket 4. sober 5. wrinkle 6. opportunity 7. pretend 8. drag
Übung 57: 1. replied 2. threw 3. won 4. grabbed 5. besought 6. paid 7. doubted 8. shrank

Übung 58: 1. The bartender offers Hudson a beer. 2. The pickpocket only pretends to be drunk. 3. The thieves ignore the law. 4. Hudson's breath smelled of whiskey. 5. He introduced himself as Matches Marconi.

Übung 59: 1. fingernail 2. predominate 3. earnings 4. reward 5. homeless 6. unnoticed Lösung: London

Übung 60: 1. nice 2. fake 3. suspicious 4. disobey 5. hurrying 6. liked

Übung 61: 1. to 2. behind 3. from 4. against 5. on 6. on 7. Until 8. since

Übung 62: 1. Verbrechen zahlt sich nicht aus. 2. Morgenstund hat Gold im Mund. 3. Es lief wie am Schnürchen.

Übung 63: 1. dig 2. empty 3. hide 4. get used to 5. lean 6. shout

Übung 64: 1. b 2. a 3. a 4. b 5. c

Übung 65: 1. literature 2. art 3. science 4. cinema 5. politics 6. music 7. cooking 8. charity 9. nobility

Übung 66: 1. protect 2. dialled 3. harmless 4. punched 5. testimony 6. announce

Übung 67: 1. a 2. b 3. a 4. b 5. b 6. a

Übung 68: 1. pretending 2. poured 3. have attacked 4. caught 5. have associated 6. had called

Übung 69: 1. richtig 2. falsch 3. richtig 4. richtig 5. falsch 6. richtig 7. falsch 8. richtig 9. richtig 10. falsch

Übung 70: 1. c 2. a 3. b 4. c

Übung 71: 1. everything 2. mistake 3. American 4. took 5. sip 6. main 7. Maybe

Übung 72: 1. insult 2. jokingly 3. laughingly 4. understanding 5. never 6. harm 7. everyday 8. ignore

Übung 73: 1. He lied about the painting. 2. Why did he pretend to be a businessman? 3. He is a master of disguise. 4. Mr Bixby and Mr Coltrane are the same person. 5. Hudson was still not satisfied. 6. Have you heard of the Phantom? 7. I have never seen his face.

Übung 74: 1. Gerücht 2. Umlauf 3. verantwortlich 4. zweifelnd 5. gierig 6. blass 7. Sicherheit 8. Grund 9. Gegenteil

Übung 75: 1. keep 2. return 3. chin 4. stole 5. attention 6. packing paper 7. fact 8. more 9. unpack 10. smiled

Übung 76: 1. Because he kept thinking about Jimmy Coltrane. 2. He was a gentlemen. He never used a weapon 3. Because he used the word 'autumn' instead of 'fall'. 4. So that they won't be afraid. 5. Lord Ploughbottom holding two dice in his hand.

Übung 77: 1. after 2. in 3. from 4. for 5. from 6. with 7. on

Übung 78: 1. jemanden auf dem Laufenden halten 2. wie ein Blitz aus heiterem Himmel 3. jemandem einen Streich spielen 4. doppeltes Spiel mit jemandem treiben 5. krumme Touren machen

Übung 79: 1. tiny/small 2. disappointingly/frustratingly 3. connection/association

4. sense/meaning 5. help/aid 6. disappear/vanish 7. bound/tied 8. pleasant/nice 9. apartment/flat

Übung 80: 1. sped 2. previous 3. owner 4. weeks 5. property 6. estate 7. drive 8. astonished

Übung 81: 1. copper 2. flawless 3. vainly 4. heir 5. bankrupt 6. estate
Lösung: Elvira

Übung 82: 1. I will inspect the old paintings. 2. He strolled out of the bank. 3. Miss Paddington had a pleasant day. 4. The real doctor was found tied to a chair. 5. When will he retire? 6. This was typical for insurance agents.

Übung 83: 1. c 2. b 3. a 4. c 5. c

Übung 84: 1. empty 2. clue, tip 3. poor, impoverished 4. constantly, regularly 5. property 6. see, note, register

Übung 85: 1. The clue in the painting was found by Hudson. 2. The car was steered by the Phantom. 3. The money was taken by the phony bank director. 4. The Ploughbottom estate is taken care of by Mr Nigma. 5. The book was picked up by Elvira.

Übung 86: 1. Verwalter 2. zittern 3. Glücksspiel 4. Anlass 5. Pech 6. Sucht 7. Umschlag 8. Tagebuch 9. Handschrift 10. verblassen

Übung 87: 1. money 2. tyre 3. heir 4. Impressionism 5. source 6. religion 7. entry 8. cover 9. secretary

Übung 88: 1. tuberculosis 2. The handwriting was different, not so shaky … 3. "*According to the rules of probability, luck must be on my side tonight.*" 4. a debt certificate 5. Isle of Man

Übung 89: 1. falsch 2. richtig 3. falsch 4. richtig 5. falsch 6. richtig 7. richtig 8. falsch 9. richtig 10. richtig 11. falsch

Übung 90: 1. loses 2. beat 3. forgive 4. devote 5. take over 6. bet 7. supports 8. grabbed 9. presents

Übung 91: 1. b 2. a 3. c 4. a 5. c 6. b

Übung 92: 1. conservative 2. dearest 3. speed 4. moustache 5. glue 6. itches

Übung 93: 1. Mr Nigma really turned out to be the Phantom. 2. No one was to be found in the salon. 3. The discovery appeared to be unbelievable. 4. Hudson could barely understand her. 5. The mobile phone went dead all of a sudden. 6. The drugs made Elvira unconscious.

Übung 94: 1. more expressive 2. younger 3. more evil 4. worse 5. best 6. richer 7. worst 8. funnier 9. more tired 10. sunnier

Übung 95: 1. jacket 2. car 3. rubber 4. television 5. kettle

Übung 96: 1. cut 2. removed 3. feel 4. fell 5. came 6. burn 7. twisted 8. passed

Übung 97: 1. furry 2. taste 3. wrist 4. stable 5. object 6. candy 7. rope 8. fist 9. lighter 10. procedure

Übung 98: 1. ballroom 2. bar stool 3. convention hall 4. couch 5. living room

6. gallery 7. health club 8. stove 9. sink 10. wardrobe

Übung 99: 1. falsch 2. richtig 3. falsch 4. falsch 5. richtig 6. richtig 7. falsch 8. richtig 9. falsch

Übung 100: 1. capital 2. hurry 3. sailor 4. kidnap 5. pant 6. dock 7. firearm
Lösung: Phantom

Übung 101: 1. elegant 2. think 3. holiday 4. conversation 5. compliments 6. way 7. approached 8. polite 9. full 10. wallet

Übung 102: 1. tasty/delicious 2. trick/cheat 3. concerned/worried 4. tell/recount 5. rest/relax 6. admiration/respect 7. signal/indicate 8. gun/firearm 9. precaution/ preventative measures 10. believe/trust 11. silhoutte/outline 12. leave/depart 13. endless/eternal 14. far/distant 15. wait/delay

Übung 103: 1. Elvira wanted to read him the diary in person. 2. The sailors stand on the dock. 3. Will you walk the entire way home? 4. Hudson used his mobile phone to book a ticket. 5. The prisoner is led into the court room. 6. The waiter will serve up the dessert.

Übung 104: 1. c 2. c. 3. b 4. a 5. b

Übung 105: 1. you 2. them 3. his 4. he 5. her 6. they 7. she 8. her

Übung 106: 1. paws 2. grace 3. backwards 4. declare 5. tempted 6. struggle 7. club 8. stranger 9. redeem 10. arrest

Übung 107: 1. Elvira's handbag 2. men's suits 3. inspectors' offices 4. James' health 5. children's stories 6. thieves' crimes 7. cell's bars

Übung 108: 1. The Pride of the Sea. 2. No. 3. That Elvira was there. 4. Take a shower and rest.

Übung 109: 1. Es hat Zeit. 2. ab und zu 3. gewaltige Anstrengungen unternehmen 4. Liebhaberwert 5. eine lange Geschichte haben 6. im wahrsten Sinne des Wortes 7. die Suppe versalzen 8. in der Familie liegen 9. auf Holz klopfen 10. wie ein Vogel im Käfig

Übung 110: 1. late 2. hope 3. case 4. mayor 5. debt 6. satisfied 7. enough 8. bad

Übung 111: 1. play it by ear 2. failsafe 3. get lucky 4. by chance 5. at sixes and sevens 6. cost an arm and a leg 7. put oneself out 8. sold up the river 9. not my cup of tea

Übung 112: 1. villain/hero 2. unscrupulous/moral 3. asleep/awake 4. rapid/slow 5. muscular/flabby 6. undecided/firm 7. restrain/release 8. smooth/uneven 9. tranquil/stormy 10. worried/carefree

Übung 113: 1. Mr Nigma attacked Elvira sincerely. 2. The Phantom possessed the debt certificate. 3. Hudson carried the gun. 4. An unknown man drugged Elvira. 5. Miss Paddington drives Elvira's car. 6. Matches Marconi will drink the beer in the dive. 7. Who will write the letter?

Übung 114: 1. b 2. a 3. c 4. b 5. b

Übung 115: 1. curls 2. comb 3. relief 4. happy 5. entire

Übung 116: 1. Can 2. May 3. Shall 4. should 5. may 6. shall 7. should 8. may 9. Can 10. Should
Übung 117: 1. richtig 2. falsch 3. richtig 4. falsch 5. richtig 6. falsch 7. richtig 8. falsch 9. richtig 10. falsch
Übung 118: 1. That there was no reception. 2. Because they were seasick. 3. He felt the Phantom still had another trump to play. 4. The mayor was to be guarded day and night. 5. He disguised himself as Elvira.
Übung 119: 1. The conversation was anything but funny. 2. Slowly, he is moving towards the table. 3. Where can I redeem this coupon? 4. Someone stepped out of the shadows. 5. Hudson will use the distraction to his own advantage. 6. We will never catch up with him! 7. He is of French ancestry.
Übung 120: 1. The waves rocked the ferry. 2. Storm clouds gathered in the sky. 3. The phoney Elvira Elliot presented the letter. 4. Are you familiar with the works of Picasso? 5. Sir Reginald wants a full report. 6. The Phantom was good looking but had a scar.
Übung 121: 1. Vermögen 2. verhindern 3. Abstammung 4. verdutzt 5. unwillkürlich 6. falsch 7. anstiften 8. lebensecht 9. Mitleid 10. Boden 11. kaum 12. verzweifelt 13. Freizeichen 14. Bericht 15. Volltreffer 16. Tagebuch 17. süchtig 18. würfeln 19. Bescheinigung 20. Ausnahme
Übung 122: 1. power 2. access 3. rose 4. sonata 5. nail 6. promote 7. staircase
Übung 123: 1. pulled 2. hissed 3. trust 4. turned 5. sprang 6. flew

Lösungen Abschlusstest

Übung 1: 1. crook 2. portrait, painting 3. chute 4. fake 5. yell, scream 6. ghost 7. dangerous 8. security 9. amazing 10. pleasant
Übung 2: 1. catch 2. made 3. leaves, will leave 4. told 5. May 6. notized 7. scribbled 8. spoken 9. will start 10. travelled
Übung 3: 1. The biscuit is eaten by Elvira. 2. Inspector Hudson saved the Isle of Man. 3. Jimmy Coltrane copied the painting. 4. By whom was the ticket for the ferry booked? 5. The car was filled with petrol by Elvira. 6. Miss Paddington read the novel.
Übung 4: 1. c 2. a 3. b
Übung 5: 1. richtig 2. falsch 3. falsch 4. richtig 5. falsch
Übung 6: 1. a, j, k 2. h, i, n 3. e, g, o 4. b, d, m 5. c, f, l, p
Übung 7: 1. avoid tax 2. render an account 3. work overtime 4. reorganize 5. compensation claim